love

jena forehand

love

LIVING WITH GOD

livingdeeper

NAVPRESS
Discipleship Inside Out®

NavPress is the publishing ministry of The Navigators, an international Christian organization and leader in personal spiritual development. NavPress is committed to helping people grow spiritually and enjoy lives of meaning and hope through personal and group resources that are biblically rooted, culturally relevant, and highly practical.

For a free catalog go to www.NavPress.com
or call 1.800.366.7788 in the United States or 1.800.839.4769 in Canada.

ISBN-13: 978-1-61291-466-4

Cover design by Lux Creative

Some of the anecdotal illustrations in this book are true to life and are included with the permission of the persons involved. All other illustrations are composites of real situations, and any resemblance to people living or dead is coincidental.

Unless otherwise identified, all Scripture quotations in this publication are taken from the *Holy Bible, New International Version*® (NIV®). Copyright © 1973, 1978, 1984, 2011 by Biblica, used by permission of Zondervan. All rights reserved. Other versions used include: the *Holy Bible*, New Living Translation (NLT), copyright © 1996, 2004. Used by permission of Tyndale House Publishers, Inc., Wheaton, Illinois 60189. All rights reserved; *THE MESSAGE* (MSG). Copyright © 1993, 1994, 1995, 1996, 2000, 2001, 2002. Used by permission of NavPress Publishing Group; The Holy Bible, English Standard Version (ESV), copyright © 2001 by Crossway Bibles, a division of Good News Publishers. Used by permission. All rights reserved; the New American Standard Bible® (NASB), copyright © 1960, 1962, 1963, 1968, 1971, 1972, 1973, 1975, 1977, 1995 by The Lockman Foundation. Used by permission; the Holman Christian Standard Bible® (HCSB), copyright © 2003, 2002, 2000, 1999 by Holman Bible Publishers. All rights reserved; the *Revised Standard Version Bible* (RSV), copyright © 1946, 1952, 1971 the Division of Christian Education of the National Council of the Churches of Christ in the USA, used by permission, all rights reserved; and the King James Version (KJV).

Printed in the United States of America

1 2 3 4 5 6 7 8 / 18 17 16 15 14 13

contents

why the LIVING DEEPER series?

I believe that deep within the heart of every woman is a desire to be part of something much bigger than herself. It's an irresistible pull to lock arms with a group of people who share a common passion that transcends the mundane rhythm of each day. This longing calls us to be part of a bigger story that involves risk and ruthless trust, because we know without God's help we are toast.

The great news is that God offers all of us these great adventures to live! The sad news is that most of us choose not to. Fear, inadequacies, insecurities, and doubt (among other things) keep us from ever experiencing life to its fullest.

In the psalms, King David penned, "Deep calls to deep" (Psalm 42:7). In song, he was expressing that the depths of God's heart continually call to the depths of ours.

God wants us to live in deeper relationship with Him. He wants to take us into the deep places where we can know Him fully, follow Him completely, obey Him willingly, and experience Him abundantly. That is what Jesus offers us: "I have come that they may have life, and have it to the full" (John 10:10).

God is ready to take us by the hand and lead us into the deeper waters of relationship with Him. He wants us to experience the exciting life He created us to live. Aren't you ready to start living deeper?

Join me and thousands of other women who are taking the plunge and heading into the deeper waters with Jesus through this guide. As we move one step at a time, we will be guided to fulfill the very purposes for which we were made. We will also be fulfilling the co-mission offered to us by Christ Himself to join Him: "Go and take others with you into the deep. Go and make disciples" (see Matthew 28:19). It was His mission and now it is ours. It's time we started really living—living deeper.

How to Use This Guide

The intent of the LIVING DEEPER series is to help women disciple others in an effective way that meets women where they are and takes them into a deeper intimacy with the Father so that they, in turn, can go and make disciples as well. We've coined the phrase, "Be a disciple. Make a disciple. Join the revolution!"

It is the Father's desire that we follow Him as a disciple, but also that we make more disciples as we go about our lives. Women all across this country are joining the team to revolutionize this world through the making of disciples, and we are thrilled that you have joined us.

Based on intensive study of how the next generation grows and learns, this book will serve as an experiential guide, combining a variety of means to help the disciple rediscover God's truths on her own through the many different mediums that she both enjoys and thrives on. It is designed to be used as a one-on-one discipleship resource or a small-group resource, keeping in mind that leading a small group also necessitates some one-on-one interaction. Though this guide provides helpful pathways and tools, it allows much flexibility, understanding that each woman leads differently and each disciple learns at her own pace. You have the freedom to follow it precisely or adapt it to the needs of the disciple or group of disciples. Ask the Holy Spirit to show you how to lead each individual, and let Him customize it specifically for her. The main goal is to faithfully disciple others in rediscovering the truth and its implications, while helping them engage God in a deeper, life-altering, and eternally transformational way.

This experiential guide is just that: a conglomeration of experiences to guide followers of Christ into applicable truth. It is broken down into weekly themes, daily nuggets that support the theme, and daily experiences that promote thought, emotion, and intent. Throughout the week, specific exercises will keep the disciple focused and meditating on the truth for that particular week.

At the end of each week, I am going to ask you to capture what you learned about who God is through a picture, song lyrics, or art. Then, I want you to bring them with you to your next time together and share those with the others in your group. It will be a fun time to get to know each other better and learn from each other all at the same time. And should anything pop up during the week, text the others in your group. It helps everyone stay committed and focused on the study as you go throughout your week.

Jesus said, "Seek and you will find" (Luke 11:9). So, as you go throughout the week, you will have daily opportunities to Seek Upwardly (What do You want me to learn, Lord? How can I apply this to my relationship with You?), Seek Inwardly (What do You want to change in my heart, Lord? How can I begin to develop this truth in my heart and life?), and Seek Outwardly (What do You want to change in my life so that I can live this truth, taking it out into the world and influencing those around me? What will I do with what You have taught me, Lord?). With each passing day, you will be growing in your relationship with God and your relationship with the others in your group (if you are in one).

As you seek, you will find, and as you find, you will realize you are living in a deeper relationship with God, and living out His love on the earth. There is no greater joy than living deeper. So what are you waiting for? Jump in!

a note from the author

Who is God?

I don't remember ever asking myself that question, because God was always a part of my family upbringing. I guess you could say I inherited God. I don't think it ever occurred to me that there were various views and understandings of God because God was defined to me by my family and church, and that was the God I believed in.

When I was on my own at college as a freshman, upperclassmen began questioning me about why I didn't do certain things. I remember my only answer was, "'Cause mama and daddy told me not to." You and I know statements like that won't fly on a college campus. It was time for me to know who I believed in, what I believed, and why I believed it, not just because my parents said so. It was time for my faith to become my own. And so I asked myself for the very first time, "Who *is* God, really?"

Some would tell you that your beliefs about God are rooted in your experiences with your earthly father. If he was kind and loving, then your view of God would be kind and loving. If he was distant and cold, then God would be distant and cold to you. Others would say that the culture or society you live in determines your definition of God. If we were honest, most of us have re-created God to be more like us. We have "humanized" Him. Most of us view God based on some form of human interaction, because that is all we have to compare Him to. And yet, no human could ever adequately, or accurately, express the fullness of the essence of who God is.

In his book *Searching for God Knows What*, Donald Miller says, "There are a lot of people who don't believe in God because they can't reconcile their idea of Him with what they see."[1] So many different people, even Christians, say so many different things about who God is—not only by their words, but by their actions—that the image of God becomes confusing, unsettling, and disillusioning.

Acts 17 records Paul's ministry in Athens as part of a missionary journey to tell the people about the one true God and Jesus Christ His Son. Speaking to the crowd gathered, Paul said, "People of Athens! I see that in every way you are very religious. For as I walked around and looked carefully at your objects of worship, I even found an altar with this inscription: TO AN UNKNOWN GOD. So you are ignorant of the very thing you worship—and this is what I am going to proclaim to you" (verses 22-23).

I began to question, "Am I worshipping a god that I created or the One True God that the Bible describes and Jesus exemplifies? Is the god I created an unknown god? Am I ignorant of the very One I worship? Is the One True God unknown to me?" And so the journey began for me to discover who God really is.

When God initiates and invites me on a journey with Him, He usually begins by speaking one word to me—just one word. At times, I have sought to figure out what the one word meant. I've attempted to create a sentence out of it and then ventured out on some course of action. Yet, I have learned over time that He is faithful to complete the sentence as we go. My only responsibility is to take Him by the hand and trust Him.

As I began on this journey to discover who He is, the Lord initiated His invitation with the word *return*. Return? Return to what? Return to who You really are?

While there is no way for me to thoroughly express all that encompasses the character of God, I will do my best to proclaim Him to you. I would invite you, too, to go on a journey with God to let Him tell you who He is. Let Him show you His true character, the One True God. Seeking to understand God as He has revealed Himself is the key to embracing Him with all of who you are.

introduction

God's people had been taken captive by the Babylonians, and the prophets were concerned. Because the Israelite people had been submerged in pagan culture, the prophets feared that the people would forget God, His covenant promise, and the response necessary to receive that promise. The prophets feared that God's chosen people would "lose their distinctiveness." This little phrase penetrated my heart.

The questions began to erupt within me: Have Christians today lost their distinctiveness? Have I lost my distinctiveness? Is there anything about me that distinguishes me in a way that others say, "There is no doubt she walks with God"? What will distinguish me?

Jesus told His disciples in John 13:34-35, "A new command I give you: Love one another. As I have loved you, so you must love one another. By this everyone will know that you are my disciples, if you love one another."

Is being distinctive *that* simple? If we love God and others the way He has loved us, we will regain our distinctiveness? The answer is a resounding *yes*.

God is love (see 1 John 4:8). Of all the words that John could have chosen to describe God, he chose the word *love*. Why? Because love is the essence of who God is. God is the author of love. God is the sum total of all love and all real love comes from God. As Creator of love,

God's love is perfect. He created it and encompasses it, and all that He does is compelled by love. Nothing He does can be done independently from His love. It is who He is. God is love.

If God is love, and if God is the originator and creator of love, then wherever authentic love is, God is. God's presence is wherever love is. Have you noticed the absence of love in today's world? Maybe this deficiency has crept in because our world has forgotten about God. Genuine love is scarce in the world because few people are experiencing the authentic love of the Father.

If God is love and we were created in His image (see Genesis 1:27), then we have the capacity to love in the same way God loves us. But we cannot give away what we do not possess. We must first understand and receive God's love so that we can give it away.

God gave us the Trinity as a means to begin to understand His character and His love. He is called Father because He knew that term would give us a frame of reference in understanding the incomprehensible depth and the fierceness of His love (see Ephesians 3:18). In love, He gave us Jesus—God wrapped in human flesh—to show us what love looks like and acts like. God knew there would be things we could not understand without a little help, so He gave us His Holy Spirit to live inside of us as a guide.

I am convinced that in order to return to the true definition of God, we must return to the presence of God. In His presence we find that all He is can be summed up in His great, unfathomable, indescribable love. As we begin to grasp the depth of His great love, we will be able to receive it and give it away. Love is the only pathway to redeem Christianity and regain our distinctiveness in the world today.

God is love. Deep, passionate, romantic, beautiful, unconditional love. The nature of His love is best understood through the picture of marriage (see Genesis 1–2). Think about it: God started His story with a marriage at creation with Adam and Eve. Then, He ends His story with Christians being with Him at the marriage supper of the Lamb (see Revelation 19:7-10; 21:9-10). Christians are called the bride of Christ (see Ephesians 5:22-23). Jesus is known as our Groom (see Mark 2:19). God speaks in marriage language so that we would recognize how He sees us—as His beloved.

God is love. Therefore, when we are in His presence, we are experiencing His love. For the next several weeks, we will learn how to live in His presence to discover who God really is—the Lover of our souls. On day 1 we will discuss what God is not. Day 2 we will delve into who God is. And days 3–5 will compel us to go into even deeper waters of this aspect of who God is. This journey you are taking with God is going to bring a freshness to your relationship with Him. It will also encourage you to let Him bust out of the box you may have put Him in and usher in a depth of knowing Him that you may not have experienced in a long time, if ever. I am so thrilled about what is going to take place as you meet with Him each day. When the time comes for meeting with your mentor or small group (I hope you have one!), don't forget to grab this study and your Bible, and be open to whatever God wants to teach you.

Get ready for the greatest journey of your life.

a match made in heaven

Day 1: God Is Not Absent

God says that the whole earth is filled with the essence of who He is (see Isaiah 6:3). The challenge throughout this study is to spend this time with God outside in nature. Sit outside or near a window and ask God to show you, through what He created, a part of who He is. Sit with Him each day and ask Him to reveal Himself to you in the creation around you. Write down how you experience God so you won't forget and so you can share your experiences with your group and encourage another. You will be amazed at what He shows you! Today, open your time with God in prayer, asking His Spirit to come alongside you and be your Teacher.

• • • • • • • • •

In our search to find out who God truly is, we can start with determining who and what He is *not*.

When I was growing up, teachers always called roll. You were marked either "present" or "absent." Too many absences brought consequences. Isn't that the same in our relationships?

If the God we know has been shaped from our experiences with our earthly father, then we may see God as absent. If you had an earthly father who was consumed with work or his own pursuits, you may feel like your father was physically and emotionally absent. After being at work all day and consumed with the stresses of the work environment, your earthly dad may have been emotionally detached and disengaged from your life and your feelings. It would be easy for you to take on this mental image of God as absent as well.

If you view God as absent, how might it make you feel? You may want to jot your thoughts in your journal.

You might believe that God doesn't care. You might think that God is only there because He is *obligated* to be there. You could believe that everything and everyone else is more important than you. If that is what you believe about God, then how might you respond to those feelings? Logically, if He doesn't care about you, then you won't care about Him or His desires for you either. The implications of misdefining God as AWOL can be catastrophic for your relationships and your future.

Believe it or not, David felt abandoned by God, too. If you have a Bible, open it up and read Psalm 22:1-2. If you don't have a Bible with you, you will always be able to read the Scripture here in the book. In your journal, record what you sense in David's emotions and his perception of God.

> My God, my God, why have you forsaken me?
>   Why are you so far from saving me,
>   so far from my cries of anguish?
> My God, I cry out by day, but you do not answer,
>   by night, but I find no rest. — Psalm 22:1-2

Psalm 22 was a prophetic psalm about Jesus and His crucifixion. Jesus even quoted from it as He hung on the cross (see Matthew 27:46). Did you notice that David and Jesus weren't questioning whether or not God existed? They *knew* God existed. That's why their cries of anguish and confusion were so deep. They knew God existed and yet they felt as though He was not coming to their rescue. God seemed absent.

Have you ever experienced a similar situation when you felt like God was absent? If so, describe it in your journal.

When both my children were babies, they cried when I dropped them off in the church nursery. They felt a sense of abandonment, of being alone. That feeling led to an anxious crying out, "Where did you go?" This is just a small parallel of the desperate cry of David and Jesus. The truth is that God had not gone anywhere, despite what they felt or experienced.

There are two different ways to understand God's presence. There is the *fact* that God is present everywhere, and then there is a *consciousness* that God is present as He reveals Himself to you. Both David and Jesus knew the reality of God's presence as encompassing all of the created world. They just didn't feel a conscious awareness of His presence. He was still very much God the Father—very aware of what was going on, where they were, and how their experiences would end in something very good.

God's perceived absence strengthened David's faith. He would later confidently say in Psalm 139:7-8,

> Where can I go from your Spirit?
>> Where can I flee from your presence?
> If I go up to the heavens, you are there;
>> if I make my bed in the depths, you are there.

David's experience as recorded in Psalm 22 developed in him a confidence that God was always there; it was just a matter of time before God would make all things right again.

When Jesus was on the cross, God could not look at all of the world's sin. Because Jesus was bearing it on that cross, He felt very alone at that moment, as God was not revealing His presence to Him. Yet three days later, He rose from the grave, and that changed everything.

Wrapping It Up

God is not an absentee Father. He may allow you to wait on Him or even feel like He has abandoned you, but He is still there. His perceived absence will result in good. Even though you do not *feel* His presence, it does not mean that He ceases to be there, any more than you not *feeling* the sun's rays means that the sun does not exist.

Loving Response

Seek Upwardly

As you begin to uncover the truth of who God really is, write these words across your journal: "God Is Not Absent." Then, take a moment to write your thoughts about what you have just learned. Maybe you need to confess that you have felt God is absent from your life. Maybe you need to repent (turn away from that thought and turn to a new way of thinking that results in different actions) of this misdefining of God and invite His help to show you who He really is.

Seek Inwardly

Ask yourself the question, "Am I absent from God? Do I make myself present with Him? How can I become more aware of His presence every moment of my life?" Talk with Him about it.

Seek Outwardly

In your journal, write this phrase from Matthew 28:20: "I am with you always." Thank God that He is not an absent Father, but that He is always with you. Carry this truth around with you today. Memorize it. You may just find that you need the reminder, or perhaps someone whose path you cross may desperately need to know this truth. Journal how this one reality changes the way you live.

Day 2: God Is Present

Head outside to sit in nature and look for God to reveal Himself to you. Invite His Spirit to teach you.

． ． ． ． ． ． ． ． ．

My husband is a twin and was notorious as a child for pulling practical jokes with his identical twin brother. Once they were in the same college class and while one left from the front of the room, the other entered from the back of the room and messed with the mind of their professor. That is, until he realized they were twins! The professor said, "I knew there was no way for you to be two places at the same time!"

God is not absent. He is present. And not just present, omnipresent. This means that God *is* everywhere at the same time. This concept is kind of hard to grasp in our minds because our thinking is confined to our own understanding of space and time. While some characteristics of God can be understood, related to, and even emulated, the omnipresence of God is not one of them. No human being can ever be omnipresent.

And though we cannot wrap our minds around His omnipresence, it doesn't cease to be true. I do not know how I can type an e-mail and press "send" and it travel across the globe. Yet I continue to do it because I know it to be true. I don't understand, but by faith, I trust it to be true.

God is not limited to time or space. If God were placed within some kind of boundaries, then He would be limited. And if God were limited, He would cease to be God. The question posed then is this: Have you put God in a box, allowing Him to be present at only certain times in your life? Not going to happen. Can't happen. God is omnipresent. He is everywhere. Even if you don't think He's there.

So why does God seem so far away, so much of the time?

Not too long ago, our family went on a mission trip to Ethiopia,

Africa. Upon meeting a group of people, we found that we were extremely limited because of our lack of communication. We could find nothing common enough for us to connect. We just sort of sat and smiled at each other. We were sitting right next to each other but felt miles apart. As the days passed, we discovered a connection: these people loved God. Though we could not understand the words they sang, when they sang them, a union of commonality transcended language. It was amazing.

Might I suggest that if you feel God is far away, it may be because you do not know Jesus Christ as Savior and Lord. This leaves you with nothing in common with a sinless God. A. W. Tozer, in his book *The Attributes of God*, speaks of this as he discusses Ephesians 2:1-3 and 4:17-19: "These verses show that the sinner is so dissimilar to God that the distance is one of character, not space. God is in perfect holiness, man perfect iniquity, and the two can never meet. That's why God seems so far away."[1]

It could also be that you are a Christian, but walking in disobedience. Second Kings 17:18 says that when God's people disobeyed Him, "the LORD was very angry with Israel and removed them from his presence." But 2 Kings 18:6-7 states that King Hezekiah "held fast to the LORD and did not stop following him; he kept the commands the LORD had given Moses. And the LORD was with him; he was successful in whatever he undertook."

God was present in both places, but Hezekiah knew the Lord was with him because Hezekiah's heart was steadfast *toward* God. There was a commonality between them. The people didn't experience God's presence because their hearts were bent *against* God. Just because they didn't feel Him didn't mean that He was not there; they simply had nothing in common with which to make a connection.

Open your Bible and read Isaiah 29:13. What does it say keeps us from an awareness of God's loving presence?

The Lord says:

> "These people come near to me with their mouth
> and honor me with their lips,
> but their hearts are far from me.
> Their worship of me
> is based on merely human rules they have been taught."
> —Isaiah 29:13

The condition of our hearts makes God seem far away. Isn't that what Isaiah 29:13 says? This verse explains that God wants to be the focus of our hearts. That's why you can even go to church and do all the right things and still feel like God is far away. If your heart is bent away from God, you'll have nothing in common with the pure heart of the Father. That's why David said,

> Who may ascend the mountain of the LORD?
> Who may stand in his holy place?
> The one who has clean hands and a pure heart,
> who does not trust in an idol
> or swear by a false god. (Psalm 24:3-4)

Wrapping It Up

If God seems far away, it is not that He has moved, but perhaps you have.

Loving Response

Seek Upwardly

Locate a small box. Keep it in a prominent place throughout this study as we will refer to it often. Set that box in front of you. Think about different things you could contain in that box—jewelry, shoes, books, money, cards, etc. Then ask yourself this question: Have you put God in a box? Are you trying to control where He can be present and where He cannot? Or does He seem so far away that you wish He were as close as that box? Do you long for His presence, and thus His love, to be revealed to you? Maybe you have thought of God as absent, uncaring, unresponsive, and unconcerned about your needs.

Seek Inwardly

Talk with Him about your feelings. Do you have enough commonalities with God to keep you connected with Him? Or do you feel as though you are not connected with Him at all? Talk about when you didn't feel His presence at certain times in your life. He is okay with your questions, your frustrations, and even your anger. He is just glad the two of you are talking. Take a little time to pour out your heart to God in your journal. Surrender yourself to let Him reveal who He really is as you journey with Him these next few weeks.

Seek Outwardly

Write "God Is Present" on a piece of paper and sit it by the box. Place the box in a prominent place so that it will often remind you of God's omnipresence, even when you don't feel Him. Record Psalm 24:3-4 in your journal. Consider ways to develop clean hands and a pure heart that has no idols, so you can stay conscious of God's presence with you. Thank God that He is always present. Ask Him to make you more aware that He is with you every day.

Day 3: God Can Be Trusted

Psalm 19:1 says, "The heavens declare the glory of God; the skies proclaim the work of his hands." As you sit out in nature today, ask your Father to declare who He is through what He created, and to speak to you as you spend this time with Him.

. . . .

I am amazed that God has always been with me, even before I was born. Psalm 139:16-18 says,

> Your eyes saw my unformed body;
>> all the days ordained for me were written in your book
>> before one of them came to be.
> How precious to me are your thoughts, God!
>> How vast is the sum of them!
> Were I to count them,
>> they would outnumber the grains of sand —
>> when I awake, I am still with you.

His presence has been and always will be with you, even while you sleep.

When I was a child, my mother would come home from work and send me outside to play while she cooked supper. She would lock the screen door and tell me to go find my own fun. We had a long, rectangular trampoline in our backyard, and I so enjoyed jumping and doing flips. But as the sun began to set and I got too tired to jump anymore, I would lie on the trampoline, prop my head up with my hands, and stare into the sky. I lay alone in the silence but I knew that God was with me. I could feel His presence.

Think about times you have felt His presence. Write down some memories in your journal.

Sometimes, God's all-present character is a hard truth to accept, especially when we remember those times when we experienced terrible things done to us. God was present for them, too. That's a tough pill to swallow. If God really loves us and God is really good, then why would He allow bad things to happen to us? And why would He stand there watching and let it happen?

The answer you'll often hear is something like this: "You were hurt because we live in a fallen world." I get that and I agree that evil resides in our world and no one is immune from it. But that still doesn't answer the main question—why God allowed that evil to happen to me! Why was I the object of someone's ridicule? Why was I labeled? Why did that person wound me so deeply? Why would God stand by silently and let this happen to me? These questions can cause a lot of anger with God and can lead you to question His love and trustworthiness.

As I have wrestled with this for most of my life, the best conclusion I have come to is this: "He knows what is best for me." Before you balk at my answer, let me share with you two stories that showed me this truth. One is my own personal experience and another is from the Bible.

When my daughter was about four years old, our family went to a place called Slippery Rock. You can slide down this God-made rock collection and land in a cold pool of water. While I recorded the event on our camera, my husband would slide down the rocks and then catch Jorja when she came down. On one of Jorja's turns, she got off the path and hit her head on one of the rocks, causing a deep puncture wound. By the time she got to the bottom, she was covered in blood. We quickly whisked her away to the emergency room where a doctor took a look at her injury. He told us that the only way to stop the bleeding was for my husband and me to take turns applying as much pressure as we could at the site of the wound. We did just what the doctor said for our daughter's sake, but it caused her (and us) great pain. She cried and cried and begged us to stop. She didn't understand why we were hurting her so much. She couldn't grasp why we had to continue it for so long. Yet, we knew it was the only way to stop the bleeding. It was for her good, even though at the time it sure didn't feel like it.

Now read a Scripture that relates to suffering. Open your Bible and read Hebrews 12:2.

> Looking to Jesus, the founder and perfecter of our faith, who for the joy that was set before him endured the cross, despising the shame, and is seated at the right hand of the throne of God. —Hebrews 12:2, ESV

According to this verse, suffering was absolutely necessary. *The Message* says, "If God didn't hesitate to put everything on the line for us, embracing our condition and exposing himself to the worst by sending his own Son, is there anything else he wouldn't gladly and freely do for us?" (Romans 8:32).

Why could God not spare His one and only Son? Why did I inflict pain on my own daughter? Because the pain was necessary.

God knows you. God made you. God knows what is best for you. He knows what lies in your future, and He allows things to teach you, mold you, and prepare you for your future. Sometimes, your greatest misery can become your greatest ministry to others. God may use the horrible experiences in your life to ignite a passion in you, a passion to create new laws, ministries, crusades, and assistance that save others from similar heartbreak.

I had a friend whose husband had an affair with her very best friend. It was a horrible experience that wounded her deeply. But after working through her emotions toward God, her husband, and others who ostracized her, she began to heal. Two years after the affair, the couple reconciled and got back together, and she was helping women who were in the same place she had been years before. Her biggest pain had become her biggest passion. She wrote me a letter telling me all about how God had helped and healed her, even after she had blamed Him and rejected Him. She ended her letter with this statement: "Now I know that my suffering was for someone else's sake." Wow.

Wrapping It Up

Your God can be trusted. Though this phrase may sound cliché, it is so true: "When you can't understand His hand, you can always trust His heart."

Loving Response

Seek Upwardly

Take out your journal and pour out your heart to God. Ask Him to reveal to you all the times that His presence was with you, even when you thought you were alone. Thank Him for always being with you, even through the hard times.

Seek Inwardly

Consider that box again. Maybe you have stored some pain away in a box and refused to talk with God about it. Talk with Him about the pain you've endured. He can handle your questions. He is actually glad you are asking. At least you are seeking Him and not running from Him.

Seek Outwardly

Record in your journal these words from Genesis 50:20, "You planned evil against me but God used those same plans for my good" (MSG). Seek to memorize this Scripture throughout the day, reminding your soul of this truth. Ask God to show you if someone you will see today needs this truth. Then share it with them as the opportunity arises.

Day 4: God, the Ultimate Matchmaker

Try to get out in God's creation today. Ask Him to reveal His presence to you and to teach you more about Him as you spend this time together.

. . . .

Have you ever heard anyone say, "This is a match made in heaven"? They have no idea what a mouthful they are saying when it comes to God!

In ancient times, Jews believed marriages were made in heaven and destined before they were even born. In *Everyman's Talmud*, the story is told of a Roman woman who asked a rabbi how long it took God to create the world. When he said it took six days, she asked him what God has been doing since then. He answered, "He has been arranging marriages."

I would like to suggest that God *has* been arranging marriages. God is a matchmaker, and He's been preparing you to meet your Husband, Jesus Christ.

We see a match being made in Genesis 24. Read the whole chapter in your Bible (or look online if you don't have a Bible handy).

God promised Abraham he would become the father of many nations. God had given Abraham and Sarah only one son, Isaac, who would bring this promise to fruition. The family born to Isaac would birth God's chosen people. When it came time for Isaac to marry, you can imagine what a big deal this was for Abraham.

What is interesting about this story is the way it parallels how God has been arranging a relationship between His Son (the Groom) and His people (us, His bride).

Note these similarities to you being the bride of Christ.

Abraham the father	God the Father
Isaac, his one and only son	Jesus, God's one and only Son
Abraham sent a matchmaker to find a bride	God sent His Spirit to prepare you to meet your Groom (see Revelation 19:7-8)

The matchmaker chose a wife for Isaac	God chose you before the creation of the world (see Ephesians 1:4)
Abraham offered a price of gifts to Rebekah	God gave Christ as the price for forgiveness
The matchmaker brought Rebekah to Isaac	The Father brought you to Christ (see John 6:44)
Isaac loved Rebekah because she was a gift from God and his father	Jesus deeply loves you because you are a gift from God (see John 17:6-10); you are His (see Song of Songs 6:3)
Isaac and Rebekah marry	You accept Christ as Savior and Lord

Now here's a neat thought: Isaac took Rebekah into his mother's tent. Why? Because Rebecca was now the one to live out God's promise for a lineage and would become fruitful. As Sarah had once been the matriarch of the family, now Rebekah would be the one reproducing and filling the tent. Likewise, once we accept Jesus Christ as our Savior and Lord, we get to live out God's promises. As He abides in us through the Holy Spirit, we become fruitful by developing the fruit of the Spirit (see Galatians 5:22-23) and by helping others know how to walk with Him (see Matthew 28:19). He wants us reproducing more Christ followers. We have been taken into the tent, so to speak, to marry our Groom and become reproducers of sorts.

Wrapping It Up

Make no mistake about it: God found His Son a bride. He found you. God, the ultimate Matchmaker, created you to be His Son's bride. He sent His Spirit to call to you, woo you, and draw you to Jesus. The price was paid, for you to be His bride. And now, Jesus waits for your answer.

Loving Response

Seek Upwardly

In your journal, write these words from Isaiah 54:5: "Your Maker is your husband."

If you have never accepted Jesus as your Savior and Lord, look in the appendix of this book to find out how you can be wed to Christ.

Take some time meditating on the truth that Jesus is the Bridegroom and you are His bride. Grab the box you used earlier this week. Sometimes boxes hold a gift inside. Imagine for just a moment that Jesus handed you this box. On a piece of paper write the words "I Choose You. Love, God." Put the words next to the box as a reminder.

Seek Inwardly

You and Jesus truly are a match made in heaven. Think about the implications of being the bride of Jesus. Use your journal to pour out your heart to Him. Talk to Him about what it means to be chosen as His.

Seek Outwardly

Who in your sphere of influence needs to hear this good news, that God chose them to be the Bride of His Son? Seek to share this with someone today.

Day 5: The With-Us God

Find another quiet place for you and God to meet out in His creation. Ask Him to speak to you as you complete this week of study.

. . . .

Think about all you have learned this week about God. How do those truths change your thinking and thus change your life?

When my family traveled to Ethiopia, we had the opportunity to visit two children we help through monthly financial support—a boy named Bereket (blessing) and a girl named Meheret (mercy). When we left them to return back home to the States, my husband said, "Those kids went from a picture to a person in one week." That is my prayer for you—that God has gone from some mental picture to a real person who deeply loves you.

In her book *Angry Conversations with God,* author Susan Isaacs described her understanding of God as the "nice Jesus on the wall," a reference to a portrait by Warner Sallman. After enduring three years of being bullied at school, she wondered why the nice Jesus on the wall didn't come to her rescue. That nice Jesus just sat there, even though she would go home from school and pray that He would do something. When He didn't respond, she eventually approached God and had an angry conversation with Him. Here is what she wrote:

Jesus: I'm so sorry you feel like I didn't come through for you. But you did know I was there; you did feel my love. Didn't you?

Susan: I did. Thank you. . . . Back then, it was the one thing I prayed for, that you'd stop Kirsten from bullying me, but you didn't answer.

Jesus: It seemed like I didn't answer.

Susan: No, Jesus. You didn't answer. Nobody came. I had to fight for myself.

Jesus: That's how I answered. I taught you to fight for yourself.[2]

So often, we miss God's presence at work in our lives, answering our prayers, because He answers them in a way we did not plan, nor expect. We "humanize" God, only expecting Him to answer as we would. But God tells us that His thoughts and ways are not our thoughts and ways (see Isaiah 55:8). He sees a much broader picture of our lives than we see. His will and ways can be trusted. He is more than a picture. He is a person. He is real, and He is intimately aware of every part of your life.

Open your Bible and read Isaiah 7:14 and Matthew 1:23. What promise is found in both verses?

Therefore the Lord himself will give you a sign: The virgin will conceive and give birth to a son, and will call him Immanuel. — Isaiah 7:14

The virgin will conceive and give birth to a son, and they will call him Immanuel (which means "God with us"). — Matthew 1:23

Wrapping It Up

Immanuel, the with-us God, has been with you all along. You may have been unaware of His presence, but He has been there nonetheless. He has been present for all the good and all the bad, and can be trusted that somehow He can use the bad for your good if only you will let Him. He is with you now. Right now. And He is not just with you in proximity. He is tuned in to you — your heart, your desires, your dreams, your pains, your fears, your hopes. He understands where your heart is at this very moment. He loves you deeply, more than words could ever express. And He gave His Son to be your Groom, your Husband—a match made in heaven. Welcome His presence as a daily, moment-by-moment reality, and let His love invade your heart. Let Him be a person instead of just a picture. He is omnipresent Immanuel. God with us.

Loving Response

Seek Upwardly

In your journal, write out your response to God. Let the truth that God is all-present and always with you sink into the depths of your heart. Pen your thanksgiving to Him.

Seek ways to remember God's presence throughout the day. For instance, set an alarm on your cell phone that offers you the reminder "I am with you" several times a day.

Seek Inwardly

Reflect on God's omnipresence. He is always with you. Always. How will that character trait of God change the way you think, feel, and act? Write out your thoughts in your journal as a reminder for future reference. Thank God for the work He is doing in you as you walk with Him in discovering who He really is.

Seek Outwardly

As you reflect on what you learned about God this week, try to capture that in a picture, song lyrics, or art. Bring your creation, along with your journal, to your next meeting so you can share all that God is doing in your heart and life.

week 2

the pursuit of happiness

Day 1: God Does Not Neglect or Reject

If you can, sit outside with the Lord today. Ask Him to reveal Himself to you as you sit in His creation. Don't rush into today's study. Be still and wait to see what He shows you. Then, invite Him to show you more of who He is as you spend this time with Him.

· · · · · · · · ·

You may have grown up in a home where both parents worked or were incredibly busy with the demands of life. Since many of us perceive our definition of God from our earthly parents, a busy parent can cause us to think that God is just too busy for us. After all, He created the world and He has to manage it. The world has become such a mess and His hands are full; therefore, we think He just doesn't have time for us.

How might those who grew up in this kind of environment feel about relationships? Write your thoughts in your journal.

You might feel abandoned. Neglected. Rejected. Those emotions are just a small step away from feeling unimportant, worthless, and unloved. What happens when you respond with those feelings toward

God? Maybe you choose to seek importance, worth, and love from those who seem to have time for you, choking out any room for God. Maybe you simply close your heart to Him since He doesn't seem to care about you anyway. This downward spiral away from God occurs because we have misunderstood who He really is.

Grab a rubber band and wrap it around the box you located last week. This is a reminder to keep this question in the forefront of your mind: "Am I closed off to God?"

In his 1974 song "Cat's in the Cradle," Harry Chapin wrote about this very busy mentality. This song describes a father who is consumed with work and too busy for his child, who grows up just like his dad. If you can, look at the lyrics to this song, because while they are directed at a parent, they illustrate how we sometimes feel about God.

This child asks, "When you comin' home, Dad?"

And the dad responds, "I don't know when, but we'll get together then; you know we'll have a good time then."

Through every season of this little boy's life, his father was totally unavailable for him. Everything else seemed more important. Promises were made, but the father never delivered on any of them. As a result, the boy grew up to be just like his dad. How sad that so much time was lost because of a father being too busy. How tragic for us if we think God is like this folk-song father and end up missing precious time with Him.

Read Psalm 27:10 and record in your journal the implications of this verse:

> Though my father and mother forsake me,
> the LORD will receive me. — Psalm 27:10

King David was saying, "Even if my father and mother neglect me, the Lord will hold me close." Webster defines the word *neglect* as "a willful lack of care and attention." Some Bible translations use the word *reject*, which is similar but it means "to set aside as inferior in quality; to refuse to accept or acknowledge." Boy, as if neglect wasn't harsh enough, reject is much worse!

So many people get no care or attention from those who ought to deeply love and care for them. Some are tossed aside as useless and worthless. They are treated as though they do not exist. If you have ever experienced someone acting as though you were invisible, you know how damaging it is. It wounds deep down in the soul, making you feel you are not worthy to be alive. It is hateful and malicious, and God never intended for anyone to be treated this way.

Rest assured that though your parents or others may not have given you the care and attention you longed for, even if they made you feel inferior and did not accept you, your God will not neglect you nor reject you. He will "hold you close." That phrase literally means "to gather you up."

Have you ever seen a child who has been separated from her mommy? What was your gut reaction? What did you want to do?

Open your Bible and read Matthew 23:37. In your journal, record Jesus' heartfelt longing.

> Jerusalem, Jerusalem, you who kill the prophets and stone those sent to you, how often I have longed to gather your children together, as a hen gathers her chicks under her wings, and you were not willing. — Matthew 23:37

Will you let Him gather you up in His arms and let Him hold you close? Why or why not? What is holding you back from the One who longs to hold you close?

Wrapping It Up

God is not a neglecting, nor rejecting Father. He longs for you to know that you are important, full of great worth, and deeply loved by

Him. And He wants to spend every waking moment with you, reminding you of that very fact.

Loving Response

Seek Upwardly

As you begin to uncover the truth of who God really is, write these words across your journal: "God Does Not Neglect or Reject." Then, take a moment to write down your thoughts about what you have just learned. Maybe you need to confess that you have felt neglected by God. Maybe you need to repent of this mistaken view of God and invite Him to show you who He really is. Also, consider how you may have been neglecting and rejecting Him.

Seek Inwardly

Write in your journal the last part of Psalm 27:10: "The LORD will hold me close" (NLT). Thank God that He does not neglect or reject you, but that He wants to give you care and attention, accepting you as important and of great worth. Carry this truth around with you today and maybe even challenge yourself to memorize it.

Seek Outwardly

Throughout the day, several people may hug you. Every time you hug them, be reminded that the Lord holds you close. You might also pray for the people you hug, that they will know that God also holds them close. If prompted, you may even whisper that truth to them. You may just find that someone whose path you cross may desperately need to know this truth.

Day 2: The Greatest Lover Pursues

Try to go outside to sit in nature and look for God to reveal Himself to you. Invite His Spirit to teach you.

. . . .

God is a Pursuer. Ponder that thought for just a moment. If God is your Husband, the greatest of all lovers, then He is obviously a pursuer, because we all pursue what and whom we love.

When my son was little, he enjoyed playing video games. I distinctly remember going upstairs one afternoon to talk to him. The whole time I was trying to get his attention, his eyes were glued to the television screen so intently that he did not even know I had entered the room. I even called out his name, but he was so consumed with the game that a train could have come through our den and he would not have known it!

The game he was playing was called "Hot Pursuit." As I sat and watched how focused, intentional, relentless, and consumed he was at his hot pursuit, I began to wonder if God was this focused, intentional, relentless, and consumed with pursuing me.

The word *pursue* means "to run after with intent; to earnestly endeavor to acquire." Throughout the Old Testament, God's people pursued their enemies to take over the land promised by God. The word was used in the context of a battle. In the New Testament, however, Jesus used the word much differently.

Read Luke 15:3-7 and discover what you learn about the Father's heart toward you.

> Then Jesus told them this parable: "Suppose one of you has a hundred sheep and loses one of them. Doesn't he leave the ninety-nine in the open country and go after the lost sheep until he finds it? And when he finds it, he joyfully puts it on his shoulders and goes home. Then he calls his friends and neighbors together and

> says, 'Rejoice with me; I have found my lost sheep.' I tell you that in
> the same way there will be more rejoicing in heaven over one sinner
> who repents than over ninety-nine righteous persons who do not
> need to repent." — Luke 15:3-7

Jesus was saying, "If a man has a hundred sheep and one of them gets lost, what will he do? Won't he leave the ninety-nine others in the wilderness and go pursue the one that is lost until he finds it?" Now the word has changed completely. The pursuit is endearing. It is intimate, focused, intentional, relentless, and consuming.

Have you ever seen a man in love? He will stop at nothing to make that girl his bride. No matter what it takes—flowers, candy, coffee, gifts, walks in the park—he will get his girl. It's a hot pursuit.

God created us to walk with Him all day, every day; yet we chose to ignore His invitation of relationship. God said to His Son, Jesus, "Son, there's Your bride. Go get her." At that very moment, Jesus began His hot pursuit of you: focused, intentional, relentless, and consumed. He was willing to do whatever it took, even death on a cross, to get His girl. It's been a passionate pursuit for your heart.

Why? Why would He pursue you with such intent? Because of love. Because you were a love gift from His Father. You are loved, not because of what you can do for Him, but simply because you are His. Think about it: Don't we only pursue what is important to us? We really only pursue what we value. What does this say about Jesus' love for you? What does it say about how much He values you?

Open your Bible and read Matthew 3:16-17. Why did God say what He did?

> As soon as Jesus was baptized, he went up out of the water. At that moment heaven was opened, and he saw the Spirit of God descending like a dove and alighting on him. And a voice from heaven said, "This is my Son, whom I love; with him I am well pleased."—Matthew 3:16-17

God claimed Jesus as His Son, proclaimed that He loved him, and exclaimed His pleasure in him. Why? Jesus hadn't performed a single miracle yet. Jesus had done nothing to earn the love and favor of God. Why did God love Him? Simply because He was His. And this is how and why Jesus loves you.

Wrapping It Up

Let this truth sink in: God has been running after you with one intent—to make you His. It has been His earnest endeavor to acquire the bride that God gave Him. And He will stop at nothing to prove His love to you.

Loving Response

Seek Upwardly

Consider for just a moment how many doors you encounter throughout the day. What if you reminded yourself each time you walked through a door or doorway, that God is relentlessly and intently knocking on your heart's door to win your love? How would that change the way you live each day? Write your thoughts in your journal.

Seek Inwardly

Now here's a tough question to ponder as we wrap up the day: Do you pursue God? Or have you closed yourself off to His pursuit and thus don't pursue Him at all? Grab another rubber band. Place the rubber band on your box and talk with God about ways you have been closing Him off, ignoring His pursuit. If someone pursues you, shouldn't you pursue him back? Shouldn't pursuit be reciprocated? Since you pursue what you value, what is important to you? What do you communicate to God if you do not pursue Him? Meditate on that for a bit and write out your heart to Him.

Seek Outwardly

Write "God Is a Pursuer" on a piece of paper and place it beside the box to remind you of this truth during the week. When you see circumstances in your life or the lives of others, consider that they may just be a means of God's pursuit. God is pursuing your happiness. The only way you will truly be happy is with Him. Encourage your friends with the truth that God will use their circumstances to remind them that He loves them and is pursuing a closer relationship with them.

Day 3: The Never-Ending Pursuit of God

As you sit out in nature today, ask your Father to declare to you who He is through what He has created, and to speak to you as you spend this time with Him.

· · · · · · · · ·

What would you say is your favorite love story of all time? Romeo and Juliet? Scarlett O'Hara and Rhett Butler from *Gone with the Wind*? *You've Got Mail*? *Sleepless in Seattle*? *Titanic*? *A Walk to Remember*? *The Notebook*? What do we like so much about these love stories? I believe it is the never-ending pursuit for the one you love.

God's pursuit of you is PERPETUAL. It never stops. It never quits. Make no mistake about it: God has been and always will be pursuing you. John 6:44 says, "No one can come to me unless the Father who sent me draws him." With every sunrise, rainbow, singing bird, answered prayer, special song, budding flower, and truth in His Word (the list could go on and on), God has been pursuing you.

Take just a minute and ask the Lord to reveal to you times that He was pursuing you over the course of your life. Record those times in your journal.

How many love stories have portrayed a hero who will not relent until he rescues the love of his life? How many women have been swept off of their feet because of the pursuit of that "special" guy? But how many women have also been disenchanted because the guy stopped pursuing her after he had won her heart? Unlike any human, God's pursuit of you never stops; it goes on and on. Forever and ever.

If God's pursuit of you and me is indeed perpetual, then why do we sometimes not feel or see His pursuit? Maybe because we have such a limited view of the ways in which Jesus pursues us. The ways I listed above only show the good gifts that are evidence of God's loving pursuit. Sometimes He also uses the painful experiences to draw us to Him.

Romans 1:23-24 says that God hands us over to do whatever our hearts desire. That doesn't feel or sound like a perpetual pursuit of a loving God! And yet it *is* a pursuit. God is jealous for you. He will not compete for your love. Nor will He have things He created take His place. In these verses, Paul described how the people began to worship the created rather than the Creator, and He was jealous. The most loving, pursuant thing their Husband could do was to hand them over to what they thought was best. He knew that in the end, they would discover that those false loves were empty and would return to their first love, the true Lover of their souls.

Has this ever been the case for you? Have you ever turned your back on God? Why or why not? How did that independence draw you back to God?

Open your Bible and read Hosea 2:6-8,14,16. What does it tell you about God's pursuit of the people He loves?

> Therefore I will block her path with thornbushes;
> I will wall her in so that she cannot find her way.
> She will chase after her lovers but not catch them;
> she will look for them but not find them.
> Then she will say,
> "I will go back to my husband as at first,
> for then I was better off than now."
> She has not acknowledged that I was the one
> who gave her the grain, the new wine and oil,
> who lavished on her the silver and gold —
> which they used for Baal. . . .
>
> Therefore I am now going to allure her;
> I will lead her into the wilderness
> and speak tenderly to her. . . .

> "In that day," declares the LORD,
> "you will call me 'my husband';
> you will no longer call me 'my master.'"
> —Hosea 2:6-8,14,16

Does fencing in with thorn bushes, blocking her path, getting her lost, and leading her into the desert sound like the pursuit of a loving God? Believe it or not, it is. God is relentless in His pursuit of you even when He allows difficult things to grab your attention. He will stop at nothing to win your heart.

In verse 14, the Hebrew word for "allure" is *pathah* and it means "to entice, seduce, persuade, flatter in silliness." God will entice, seduce, persuade, and even flatter you to win you back. Your Husband is on a pursuit for your heart to be the sole recipient of your love.

Once He gets your undivided attention, He speaks "tenderly" to you (Hosea 2:14). That word means that He speaks His deep love into the depths of your heart, your mind, your emotions, and your desires. This is not a casual relationship. His desire is for deep, deep intimacy.

Wrapping It Up

God has been pursuing you since before you were born. He made you and loves you more than any other could. His pursuit is perpetual. It never ends. No matter how far you run from Him, He will relentlessly pursue you. This is a love story like no other: a Lover who will stop at nothing to win the object of His love.

Loving Response

Seek Upwardly

Can you think of times in your life when God allowed you to go your own way so that you would find that He is all you need? Did you experience times when He walled you in to draw you in with His love? What did it look like? How did you respond? Did He win your love or did you continue to run from Him? Where are you with Him today?

Seek Inwardly

Take some time to share your heart with God. Journal if you want. Sit in the quiet and let your Husband speak tenderly to you. Write down in your journal whatever He says to you. Then summarize it on a piece of paper and place it by your box so you can refer to it again and again.

Place another rubber band around your box and talk with the Lord about why you might be closed off to His perpetual pursuit.

Seek Outwardly

Draw a picture of a clock in your journal. Beside it, write "God's Pursuit Is Perpetual" and look for His loving pursuit throughout the day. Even while writing this, I saw one of the most beautiful skies ever, and I heard the Lord say, "I sure do love you." Write down or capture in a picture the ways God lovingly pursues you through the seemingly good and bad of life.

Day 4: The Progressive Pursuit of God

Try to go outside again today or sit near a window and take in all the gifts that God gives you as He pursues you.

• • • • • • • • •

First, it's a glance. Then, a smile. Then, the greeting. I'll never forget when I met my husband. He introduced himself like he was Elvis Presley, all suave and debonaire. I acted as though it was no big deal, but inside, I was secretly ecstatic! With most relationships, there is a progression. God's pursuit of us is much the same.

God's pursuit is PROGRESSIVE. It grows over time. God wants to move toward deeper intimacy with you. Yesterday, you learned that God's pursuit of you is perpetual. This unending pursuit confirms that His love is undying and eternal. This unending wooing causes us to pursue Him in return. God desires to be pursued just like we do. And the more He pursues and we pursue in return, the more progress is made in the relationship.

This progression of intimacy in our relationship with God is reflected in Scripture.

Open your Bible and read Isaiah 64:8. What kind of relationship is indicated here?

> Yet you, LORD, are our Father. We are the clay, you are the potter; we are all the work of your hand. — Isaiah 64:8

In Scripture, our relationship with God is often described in terms of the POTTER AND CLAY. He gently molds our hearts with His loving hands until our hearts look like His. However, this relationship isn't very intimate. The potter doesn't share his dreams or desires with the clay. He molds it.

Read John 10:14-15 and look for the relationship analogy used here.

> I am the good shepherd; I know my sheep and my sheep know
> me — just as the Father knows me and I know the Father — and I lay
> down my life for the sheep. — John 10:14-15

Jesus echoed David's analogy in Psalm 23 of SHEPHERD AND
SHEEP. He called Himself the Good Shepherd and His people the
sheep. In this understanding, God leads us. We know His voice and
follow Him, and He lovingly protects us and guides us along in the
right path.

Then, a few chapters later, Jesus used another word picture to
describe our relationship with God. Read John 15:13-15 to discover
the analogy He used.

> Greater love has no one than this: to lay down one's life for one's
> friends. You are my friends if you do what I command. I no longer call
> you servants, because a servant does not know his master's business.
> Instead, I have called you friends, for everything that I learned from
> my Father I have made known to you. — John 15:13-15

In this instance, Jesus talked about His followers NOT AS
SERVANTS BUT AS FRIENDS. Friends do life together. They
share everyday experiences along with life-changing ones. They laugh
together and cry together, sometimes simultaneously. Friends can
share deep, healthy intimacy, but even that is insufficient compared to
how God longs to relate to His people.

To describe this most unique and sacred relationship, Scripture
uses the terms BRIDE AND BRIDEGROOM. Read Revelation
19:6-9 and use your creative talents to create a picture in your journal
that shows what you read.

Then I heard what sounded like a great multitude, like the roar of rushing waters and like loud peals of thunder, shouting:

"Hallelujah!
    For our Lord God Almighty reigns.
Let us rejoice and be glad
        and give him glory!
For the wedding of the Lamb has come,
        and his bride has made herself ready.
Fine linen, bright and clean,
        was given her to wear."
(Fine linen stands for the righteous acts of God's holy people.)

Then the angel said to me, "Write this: Blessed are those who are invited to the wedding supper of the Lamb!" And he added, "These are the true words of God." — Revelation 19:6-9

What a beautiful picture — a wedding. A bride dressed in the purest of white linens. A husband waiting to be joined with his beloved. The look of longing between them. A celebration. A consummation, a union, a covenant pledge of love. No greater intimacy exists than between the beloved and her husband.

Do you see the progression? God wants to date you, woo you, be united with you. He is pursuing you relentlessly, for the purpose of making you His very own. What is required, by God and you, for this progression to take place?

His presence. In order for Him to mold you as a Potter, guide you as a Shepherd, relate to you as a Friend, and wed you as a Bridegroom, He must be in your presence to do so! We have already discovered that He is always present. But in order for you to be engaged in the progression, you have to be fully aware of His presence working in you and through you. And since God is love, then wherever His presence is, His love is. It is that perfect love that draws you into deeper intimacy with Him.

Wrapping It Up

God's pursuit of you is progressive. His part is His loving presence. Your part is awareness and surrender. In order for the progression to take place, you must be willing to relinquish control of yourself to God. Think about it: a Potter can't mold without "surrendered" clay. A Shepherd can't guide without "surrendered" sheep. A Friend can't reveal Himself to you without a "surrendered" ear. And a Groom certainly can't wed His Bride without a "surrendered" heart.

Loving Response

Seek Upwardly

Where do you find yourself with God, the Lover who has been perpetually and progressively pursuing you? Are you stuck somewhere in your relationship with God? Where? Why? Have you limited God's progressive pursuit of you? Place one last rubber band on your box and talk with the Lord about where you are in relationship with Him.

Seek Inwardly

Draw a white flag of surrender in your journal. Write a letter to the Lord about your feelings regarding surrender. Tell Him you want to go deeper in relationship with Him, and ask Him to take you there. As an act of surrender, write that word in the center of your flag with this psalm below it: "And those who know your name put their trust in you, for you, O Lord, have not forsaken those who seek you" (Psalm 9:10, ESV). God wants you to put your trust in Him and let Him carry you into deeper relationship with Him. He will not forsake you when you seek Him.

Seek Outwardly

Make a white flag of surrender or write the word *surrender* on a card. Sit it in a prominent place as a reminder that God is present and needs your surrender in order to take you into a deeper relationship with Him. Look for opportunities to share this with another.

Day 5: The Purposeful God

Reflect on these words: "They know the truth about God because he has made it obvious to them. For ever since the world was created, people have seen the earth and sky. Through everything God made, they can clearly see his invisible qualities—his eternal power and divine nature" (Romans 1:19-20, NLT). Now go out in nature today and ask God to make Himself obvious to you through all that He has made.

• • • • • • • • •

Have you ever "buttered someone up"? You know, you are kind and serving and giving because you need them to do something for you? Most everything we do is for a purpose. There is a motive. Something is always driving us.

God's pursuit is PURPOSEFUL. Can you ever think of a time when you pursued something or someone for no reason? No! We pursue what we value for a reason.

So it is with God. If that's the case, what is the purpose of God's perpetual, progressive pursuit of us?

I would like you to consider two Scriptures that I believe indicate the ultimate purpose for God's relentless pursuit of us.

Open your Bible and read John 3:16 and John 10:10. Discover the common theme in both.

> For God so loved the world that he gave his one and only Son, that whoever believes in him shall not perish but have eternal life. —John 3:16
>
> The thief comes only to steal and kill and destroy; I have come that they may have life, and have it to the full. —John 10:10

So often, we think that John 3:16—many times the first verse we memorize and the verse that sums up the gospel—is speaking of eternal life, which it is. However, we *only* think of eternal life in terms of what we receive *after* we die.

In reality, both Scripture verses say that Jesus came for the sole purpose of giving you and me life, eternally and abundantly. That word *life* is *zoe,* and it means "excitement; animation; life that is real and genuine, a life active and vigorous, devoted to God, blessed; superior in quality and superabundant in quantity." *That's* the life that Jesus came to give us! This truly is the pursuit of happiness. This is the purpose of His pursuit. And He offers that now, not just when we die. The word *eternal* in John 3:16 means "never-ending; without beginning and end, that which always has been and always will be." And what have we already learned that has always been and will always be? God's presence.

God's purpose for pursuing you is so that you can live life in His presence, in His love. From the very beginning, God created you to walk with Him. The Bible tells us that Adam and Eve walked with God in the cool of the day. Enoch walked with God. Abraham walked with God. God wants us to walk with Him so that He can love on us, show us who He truly is, and tell us who we are and who He made us to be. He desires for us to continue to walk with Him as we learn how to live out His will for us in daily life. He knows what is best because He made us, so we walk closely to Him as He molds us, guides us, reveals Himself and His will to us, and weds us as we become completely His. This is the gospel, the too-good-to-be-true news.

Wrapping It Up

God is your pursuer because you are worth pursuing. His love propels Him to pursue you perpetually, progressively, and purposefully. He created you to walk with Him in deep communion and experience the *zoe* life He died to give you. Don't settle for anything less.

Loving Response

Seek Upwardly

How does what you have learned this week change your thinking and thus change your life?

Take some time to look at your box. Have you kept such a tight lid on your heart that you have refused to let God love you? Cut the rubber bands off your box. Maybe you need to cut loose your heart and allow God to pursue you (and you pursue Him in return). Place the cut rubber bands in your box as a reminder to allow your Husband to pursue you. It truly is the only pursuit of happiness.

Let the truth that God is pursuing you sink into the depths of your heart. In your journal, pen your thanksgiving to Him. Watch for God's pursuit of you. When situations come your way, begin to ask God, "Is this You pursuing me?" Ask God to make you alert to His pursuit of you.

Seek Inwardly

Reflect on God as the Pursuer. How will this trait of God change the way you think, feel, and act? Record your thoughts in your journal as a reminder. Thank God for the work He is doing in you as you walk with Him, discovering who He really is.

Seek Outwardly

Record John 3:16 in your journal. Seek to memorize it. Look for times when you can share with a friend about God's desire to walk with them, offering a vibrant exciting life in His loving presence.

As you think about what you learned about God this week, try to capture that in a picture, song lyrics, or art. Bring it, along with your journal, to your next meeting so you can share all that God is doing in your heart and life.

week 3

tying the knot

Day 1: God Is Not a Game-Player

Sit outside or near a window and ask God to show you, through what He created, a part of who He is. His character shows up in all that He created. Write it down so you won't forget and so you can share it with your group and encourage others. You will be amazed at what He shows you!

· · · · · · · · ·

Soap operas have been a staple in America since the early 1950s. Continual episodes of various story lines interwine deception, betrayal, greed, lust, love, and more. These afternoon dramas offer something intriguing, even alluring. They have become, for many, an escape from their mundane and "drama-less" lives, taking them into a fantasy world that they could imagine as real. Though many may say they would like to live "drama-less" lives, they miss not "feeling" anything. So, in an effort to feel, they "create" drama in their lives so that at least they will feel something.

Have you ever met people who play games in a relationship? They are always starting drama, always yanking on your emotions, always sending you on an exhausting and sickening roller coaster. Their motive is completely selfish: to keep stringing you along, trying to keep you engaged, trying to make you stay with them, trying to make themselves the center of attention. They always seem to time their drama when you are leaving to go out of town so that you will be miserable while you are gone. That is what they want! They want to punish you because you left them back home. One minute they want to be with you, and the next, they don't. If you have been treated like this in relationships, how easy it would be for you to take on this mental image of God.

If you view God as a game-player, how might you feel? Record your thoughts in your journal.

You might think He is sitting on the throne in heaven, moving your life around like a pawn in a chess game, watching how you will respond to the things He places in your life. You might feel jerked around. Toyed with. At the mercy of His capricious whims. If that is how you feel, how might you react to God? If He is going to put you on the roller coaster of emotions and drama, wouldn't you just rather get off the ride? Or if He is going to play games with you, then maybe you will just play games with Him? The results of this misconception of God as nothing but a game-player can make a mess of your relationships now and in your future.

Think for a minute about Moses. God called to him from a burning bush to go to Egypt and bring His children out of Pharaoh's tyranny. But in the conversation, God told Moses that Pharaoh would not listen. Over and over, through some of the worst plagues ever, he would still be stubborn and refuse to relent. Now this is not what we would consider a pep talk! But Moses did what was asked of him, only to find that God's people didn't believe him and even got angry at him because Pharaoh put more and more hardship on them. Do you think that at any time, Moses might have thought, "Lord, what are you doing? Is this some sick game you are playing with me? With your people? What is up?!" I think it would be a legitimate question.

Read Exodus 5:22-23 and note what Moses said to God.

Moses returned to the L ORD and said, "Why, Lord, why have you brought trouble on this people? Is this why you sent me? Ever since I went to Pharaoh to speak in your name, he has brought trouble upon this people, and you have not rescued your people at all."
—Exodus 5:22-23

God replied with several reassurances in the following chapters: "I have promised to rescue you from your oppression in Egypt. I will lead you to a land flowing with milk and honey" (Exodus 3:17, NLT).

"I will make Pharaoh's heart stubborn so I can multiply my miraculous signs and wonders in the land of Egypt" (Exodus 7:3, NLT).

"I've also done it so you can tell your children and grandchildren about how I made a mockery of the Egyptians and about the signs I displayed among them—and so you will know that I am the L ORD" (Exodus 10:2, NLT).

Basically, God said that He would do what He promised, but challenged Moses to trust Him because it would take some time; the time was a necessary component for the people to see and be convinced that He is God; He wanted them so convinced that they would share this conviction about God to the generations that would follow.

Could it be that God is trying to do the same thing in your life? That He wants you to trust Him even if the timing is not to your liking? Maybe He wants you to trust that His timing is a necessary component to the overall picture. Perhaps the waiting provides the opportunity for others to be convinced and to tell future generations about who He is and what He can do.

Wrapping It Up

When you begin to walk with God, He will take you on a journey that beats any soap opera. After all, He's been planning it since before you were born! However, when questions arise in the midst of the journey, we must learn to trust that He is working out His plan in perfect timing. Time truly is a necessary component to completing the overall purposes for which you were made. You must trust that God is not a game-player, but an implementer in His well-thought-through plan.

Loving Response

Seek Upwardly

As you begin to return to the truth of who God really is, write these words across your journal: "God Is Not a Game-Player." You may even want to draw a chess piece (like a pawn) and put a big X over it. Then, take a moment to write your thoughts about what you have just learned. Maybe you need to confess that you have felt this way toward God. Maybe you need to repent of misdefining God and invite Him to show you who He really is.

Seek Inwardly

Take some time to ponder this question: Do you play games with God? Confess your game-playing and seek His forgiveness.

Write these words from Psalm 33:4: "For the word of the LORD holds true, and we can trust everything he does" (NLT). Thank God that He is not playing games with your heart, but that He can be trusted.

Seek Outwardly

Carry this truth with you today and maybe even memorize it. You may just find that you need the reminder, or someone whose path you cross may desperately need to know this truth. Others need to know that God is not playing games with their lives or heart. You may be the one who can share that truth with them.

Day 2: God Is a Promise-Keeper

Try to get outside to sit in nature and look for God to reveal Himself
to you. Invite His Spirit to guide you into His truth.

• • • • • • • • •

I can remember making promises to my friends as a child. We would
tell who we thought was the cutest guy at school, but we didn't want
anybody else to know. We quoted this little phrase to show we would
keep the secret: "Cross my heart; hope to die; stick a needle in my
eye." It was a serious promise, because I certainly had no intentions of
sticking a needle in my eye!

We long for relationships that are stable and promise-keeping. We
want our friends and family to be committed and trustworthy to the
very end. Since we are created in the image of God, He desires committed relationships, too. Therefore, God made a public display of His
loyalty to us and proved Himself to be a Promise-Keeper. His proof?
The birth, death, and resurrection of His only Son, Jesus.

The Old Testament (*testament* means "covenant") records two
kinds of covenants (or promises): those made by a man to another
man, and those made by God to a man. God made promises to Adam,
Noah, Abraham, Moses, and David. He is a covenant-making God.
One such covenant is found in Genesis 15, when God makes a covenant with Abraham.

Read Genesis 15 and Genesis 17 and record what you learn about
God's covenant to Abraham (called Abram early in this encounter).
List in your journal anything new you'd never noticed before.

This covenant involved several elements:

Sacredness

"The Lord spoke to Abram in a vision and said to him, 'Do not be
afraid, Abram, for I will protect you, and your reward will be great'"
(Genesis 15:1, NLT). With reality television, YouTube, Facebook, and
Twitter, it seems as though nothing is sacred anymore. The word

sacred means "worthy of dedication and respect; declared and believed as holy."[1]

Two very sacred moments occurred in my life at the birth of my children; their births were holy, reverently awing experiences. Those moments were so difficult to explain in words: humbling, awesome, godly. By the time they were six weeks old, my husband and I stood before our faith family (church) and in a special ceremony, we made a covenant to raise each one to know and make known the love of God, His Son, Christ Jesus, and the Holy Spirit. This dedication was a big deal to me; it was a calling out, filled with purpose and promise. It gave me a sense of worth, that I could actually make a difference in the life of another.

God's covenant to Abraham was no different. It was a sacred moment, initiated by the Creator of the Universe. And He has offered His covenant with you. The Creator of the Universe loved you enough and deemed you worthy enough to make a public display of loyalty to you. And each time you hear His voice guiding you, He is keeping His covenant with you. Think on that for a moment. The Bible calls that "Selah," which means "reflective pause."

Sacrifice

Did you ever prick your finger to make your friend and you "blood sisters"? Not me! I was way too chicken! And I was certainly not going first. I needed some proof that she would make the same sacrifice of pain.

In the covenant between Abram and God, several animals were sacrificed—a three-year-old heifer, a three-year-old female goat, a three-year-old ram, a turtledove, and a young pigeon. Why use three-year-old animals? In biblical numerology, the number three denotes completion. God used this to affirm His faithfulness to keep His promise.

That evening, Abraham had a dream. In that dream, he saw a smoking pot and a flaming torch passing between the two pieces of the sacrifices. I would like for you to consider that the smoking pot represents death to self as the flesh is burned. You can't fulfill your end of the covenant if you live by your flesh, trying to do it on your own. I believe the flaming torch represented the presence of God to guide us. You can't fulfill your end of the covenant if you won't let God lead you. The message of the blood sacrifice was communicating, "May it be done to you as it was done on this altar (death) should you not keep your end of the covenant." That's a powerful oath. Make no mistake about it: making covenant with God will require sacrifice—a sacrifice of your flesh and a sacrifice of control so that God can lead.

Specifics of the Couenant

In Genesis 17, God reaffirmed His covenant with Abram to make Him the father of many nations. God also set forth the specifics of the covenant—the responsibilities each would fulfill. Both parties had a part to play. Both had to agree to the terms, and both had to commit to them forever. And again, if one chose to break the covenant, death was the result. Covenant is serious business.

Spoken Vows

In Genesis 17, God voiced His vows to Abraham. God promised to make Abraham the father of many nations.

There is something sacred about a person looking you in the eye and making a promise to you. Growing up, I was told, "Your word is your honor; it may kill you, but you will do what you said you would do. If you don't have honor and integrity, you have nothing." Today, unfortunately, verbal promises mean nothing. I witnessed a man, overcome by sexual addiction, tearfully re-marry his wife, giving rings not only to her but his two daughters, promising to never leave them, to be the dad they need, and to never let them down. He didn't keep his promises. Ecclesiastes 5:5 says, "It is better not to make a vow than to make one and not fulfill it." God verbally spoke His commitment to Abraham, and He kept every word of it.

Showering of Gifts

Gifts given during a covenant were sometimes called the Seal of the Covenant. In biblical times, when someone purchased a large amount of items at the market, he did not have the means to lug all of his loot home. Therefore, he would bundle all of it up and melt wax onto the outer wrapping to hold the bundle closed. Then, the man would press his signet ring into the melted wax to show ownership. He was the only one who was allowed to break the seal and have the treasures inside. Gifts were given to "seal the deal," showing proof that a covenant had indeed been made. God's gift to Abraham was changing his name (see Genesis 17:5). Abraham means "father of many." Abraham's new name matched his new calling.

Signs

God wanted the world to know that Abraham and his offspring were His, so He required them to bear a mark separating them out as His chosen people. The sign was circumcision:

> This is the covenant that you and your descendants must keep: Each male among you must be circumcised. You must cut off the flesh of your foreskin as a sign of the covenant between me and you.... All must be circumcised. Your bodies will bear the mark of my everlasting covenant. Any male who fails to be circumcised will be cut off from the covenant family for breaking the covenant. (Genesis 17:10-11,13-14, NLT)

Sharing a Meal

Sometimes, by way of commemorating and celebrating a covenant, the two parties would enjoy a meal together. Breaking bread together was highly symbolic of relationship. Often, people broke bread in their homes, sharing the same table. Or, you might even get the privilege of sitting at the King's table. Sharing the same table was a symbol of covenant.

Wrapping It Up

When you study God's covenant made with Abraham—the tying of the knot—and all the elements involved, you can begin to see the similarities of an earthly marriage covenant. You must also grasp the understanding that our spiritual covenant and union with God through Jesus have these same elements as well. God wants to tie the knot with you in covenant. Covenants are serious. God takes His covenant with you seriously. Do you?

Loving Response

Seek Upwardly

Journal what the Holy Spirit revealed to you today. Record this Scripture from Hebrews 10:23: "God can be trusted to keep his promise" (NLT). Your deeply loving Groom has offered to make a very serious and sacred covenant with you. How does that make you feel? How might it change the way you live each day? Write down your thoughts. Write "God is a Promise-Keeper" on a piece of paper and stick it in your box to remind you of this truth during the week.

Seek Inwardly

Dialogue with God about today: Do you take your covenant with God seriously? Why or why not? How can you begin to reciprocate your covenant with God?

Seek Outwardly

Another way we made promises as kids was to make "pinky promises." Take a permanent marker and write the word *covenant* on your pinky finger, reminding you that God is a promise-keeping God and you must remember the promises you made to Him.

Day 3: The Promise of Jesus

As you sit out in nature today, ask your Father to declare to you who He is through what He created and to speak to you as you spend this time with Him.

• • • • • • • • •

Yesterday, we looked at the elements of the covenant between Abraham and God. Today, I want us to examine the similarities between the Old Testament covenant with Abraham and the New Testament covenant, found in Jesus.

Sacredness

"The Word became flesh and made his dwelling among us. We have seen his glory, the glory of the one and only Son, who came from the Father, full of grace and truth" (John 1:14). "And she gave birth to her firstborn son and wrapped him in swaddling cloths and laid him in a manger, because there was no place for them in the inn" (Luke 2:7, ESV).

The birth of our Savior was so sacred. There was nothing sacred about the place; it was the presence of the Person that made it sacred. No greater gift has ever been given: Jesus, Savior of the world. Born in a manger. Born to die for us. Is there anything more humbling, more awe-inspiring, more beautiful? What kind of love is this? God came to earth to show us how to live and then gave His life so we could live.

Today, we celebrate His birth on Christmas, yet how "un-sacred" it has become. The birth of Jesus gets shoved to the back burner with sales at the mall, company parties, traveling to family gatherings, and Santa Claus. In the hustle and bustle of the holidays, sometimes the birth of our Savior is not even mentioned. Many people are even trying to remove His name altogether, forcing businesses, schools, and media outlets to say "Happy Holidays" instead of "Merry Christmas." Jesus, God in the flesh, left the majesty of heaven to be born in a cattle trough. Oh, what love. What a truly sacred moment.

This is the New Covenant. It is the heart of the gospel: Sin (our choosing to walk away from God instead of with Him) separated us from God, resulting in our punishment of eternal separation in a real place called hell. But Jesus stepped in and took the punishment on our behalf. We are His bride, given to Him by God. He would do anything to save the love of His life. Anything. And so He died in order for you and me to truly live—to live the life that God intended when He created us. We were pronounced "not guilty," reconciled to our Creator, Father God. Jesus was sent to save His bride. And He did.

Sacrifice

"Without the shedding of blood there is no forgiveness" (Hebrews 9:22). God provided an example of this truth beginning with Adam and Eve when He covered their nakedness with a sacrificed animal. We think God slaughtered the animal, washed it off, laid it out to dry, cut out a pattern of a coat, and then placed it on Adam and Eve. That would have taken many days. Many believe that is not what happened at all. They suggest that He sacrificed an animal and laid the warm, bloody fur over them. This aligns with the Scriptures that say without the shedding of blood, there is no forgiveness for our sin. That sacrificial death covered their sin and restored them back to God. Just as the covenant with Abraham required a sacrifice, annual blood sacrifices made atonement for people's sin throughout the history of God's people, the Israelites. All of this was a foreshadowing of the new and better covenant that would be made through Jesus' sacrifice for you and me.

"It can never, by the same sacrifices repeated endlessly year after year, make perfect those who draw near to worship" (Hebrews 10:1).

"It is impossible for the blood of bulls and goats to take away sins" (Hebrews 10:4).

"We have been made holy through the sacrifice of the body of Jesus Christ once for all" (Hebrews 10:10).

"Let us draw near to God with a sincere heart and with the full assurance that faith brings, having our hearts sprinkled to cleanse us from a guilty conscience" (Hebrews 10:22).

"Christ is the mediator of a new covenant" (Hebrews 9:15). Jesus' death was the only way for God to make a new covenant with us, bridging the gap that separated us. That's why Jesus is often called "The Lamb of God." He was the only perfect Lamb able to be the sacrifice for our sin (see John 1:29). Second Corinthians 5:21 says, "God made him who had no sin to be sin for us, so that in him we might become the righteousness of God."

How should we respond to such a deeply loving and selfless sacrifice? By offering our lives completely to Him. Jesus said, "Whoever wants to be my disciple must deny themselves and take up their cross and follow me" (Matthew 16:24). Paul challenged us to present our bodies as a living sacrifice; this is the only reasonable thing we can do in response to Jesus' sacrifice (see Romans 12:1). Paul later went on to say, "I have been crucified with Christ and I no longer live, but Christ lives in me. The life I now live in the body, I live by faith in the Son of God, who loved me and gave himself for me" (Galatians 2:20). A crucified life of love is the least we can do for what He has done for us.

Specifics of the Covenant

This new covenant had new terms. Under the Old Covenant, the conditions were stated as "If you do this, then I will do this." Under the New Covenant, there are no conditions but simply, "I have freely done this, so out of a heart of gratitude, do this." Jesus made His covenant with us without any conditions. He gave Himself as an unwarranted gift to you, His bride. We call this grace. His unconditional love compelled Him to give His life for us so we could be with Him forever. And all He asked from us was this: "A new command I give you: Love one another. As I have loved you, so you must love one another" (John 13:34). Jesus was even asked by the keepers of the Old Covenant (who refused accepting Him as the mediator of the

New Covenant) to cite the greatest of all the laws given (see
Matthew 22:34-40). Jesus answered, "'Love the Lord your God with
all your heart and with all your soul and with all your mind.' This is
the first and greatest commandment. And the second is like it: 'Love
your neighbor as yourself.' All the Law and the Prophets hang on
these two commandments" (verses 37-40). Why was His answer
love? Why does everything hang on love? Why is love our response
to His gracious gift? Because God is love. All that He does is moti-
vated by love. Love compelled God to send His Son to die for us.
Love caused His Son to die for you, His bride. God is love.

The word *hang* means "depend." Jesus was saying that all behavior depends upon being done in love. Because of His great love for us,
our only response is to offer love in return, both to Him and to
others—reciprocated love to Him, unwarranted love to others (just as
He gave).

Spoken Vows

Jesus said, "Do not let your hearts be troubled. You believe in God;
believe also in me. My Father's house has many rooms; if that were
not so, would I have told you that I am going there to prepare a place
for you? And if I go and prepare a place for you, I will come back and
take you to be with me that you also may be where I am" (John 14:1-3).
He looked at His disciples and made them this promise. Jesus died for
our sins, conquered death, was raised to life, and ascended back to His
Father so that we could have new life through Him and live forever
with Him. He made a vow and He will be faithful to keep His
promise.

Showering of Gifts

"Praise be to the God and Father of our Lord Jesus Christ, who has
blessed us in the heavenly realms with every spiritual blessing in
Christ" (Ephesians 1:3). The gifts granted us in the covenant are too
numerous to discuss. Grace, mercy, eternal life, heaven, strength,

hope, and more were all included as gifts of the covenant. But one of the greatest gifts given to us is the gift of His Holy Spirit living in us.

Read Ephesians 1:13-14 and record what you find about this amazing gift of the Holy Spirit.

> And you also were included in Christ when you heard the message of truth, the gospel of your salvation. When you believed, you were marked in him with a seal, the promised Holy Spirit, who is a deposit guaranteeing our inheritance until the redemption of those who are God's possession — to the praise of his glory. — Ephesians 1:13-14

Jesus, your Groom, placed His seal of ownership on you. This seal signified a final transaction and the confident security that He would return to get His bride.

So what is your gift in return? Read Acts 11:26 and find out.

Obedience, prayer —

> And when he [Barnabas] found him [Saul], he brought him to Antioch. So for a whole year Barnabas and Saul met with the church and taught great numbers of people. The disciples were called Christians first at Antioch. — Acts 11:26

At salvation, not only did you receive the Holy Spirit, but your name was changed to Christian. That word means "little Christ," a smaller but accurate replica of Jesus. Your gift to Jesus in return is to represent Him accurately. God is love. Jesus is love. To replicate Jesus is to love others. That's why His new command was to love as He has loved. Just before His death, Jesus said, "A new command I give you: Love one another. As I have loved you, so you must love one another. By this everyone will know that you are my disciples, if you love one another" (John 13:34-35).

Signs

Jesus bore the marks of the covenant—His nail-scarred hands and feet. By these, the world would know of His undying love and the lengths He would go to have you as His own.

God wants the world to know that you are His, but He no longer requires you to bear the physical mark of circumcision. Instead, He desires circumcised hearts (see Deuteronomy 10:16; 30:6; Romans 2:28-29), cutting away our selfishness and allowing the Holy Spirit to help us love as He loves. That is why His gift was His Spirit inside of us. He knew that we would be incapable of loving as He loves without His help. The Holy Spirit is our comforter (see John 14:16), our guide to all truth (see John 16:13), our Counselor (see John 14:26), and more. The mark of His bride is a circumcised heart pouring out God's love, by the help of the Holy Spirit.

Sharing a Meal

Jesus brought His disciples to a table, a sign of the covenant, to have their last meal together (see Luke 22:7-20). The bread represented His body broken for many. The cup represented His own blood poured out to cover sin.

Here is the beauty of the covenant table: The way people reclined at a table in Jesus' day meant that their bodies were almost completely covered so all that really showed was their face. The table represents how the covenant, made by God through Jesus to us, covers us completely, not showing any unclean parts. The covenant meal was placed on that table and all who reclined around it were given the right to eat.

There is a story in the Bible about a man named Mephibosheth (see 2 Samuel 9). He was crippled in both legs, yet was invited to eat at King David's table. I would like to suggest that the table of the covenant covered his imperfections and gave him the freedom to dine with the king. How thankful I am that the King of Kings took the punishment for my sin and invited me to His table where my sin is covered by His blood. Because of His sacrifice, you and I can come and dine with Him in deep communion and intimate relationship.

The next time you partake of communion at the Lord's table, may you remember the love that your Groom had for you—a love so deep that He was broken and poured out so He could have you as His very own, forever. Communion is to be treated with great sacredness. It is His table that covers everything, and it will surely cover you. My favorite line in the song "Seek Me" by Watermark captures this idea so well: "'Cause my table covers everything, it will always cover you."[2]

Wrapping It Up

I know your heads may be spinning with all the information packed in these days! I pray that the Holy Spirit has used this to incite you to study for yourself the correlations and foreshadowing between the Old Covenant of the Law and the New Covenant of Grace through Jesus Christ.

Loving Response

Seek Upwardly

Take some time to ask yourself these questions and discuss them with your Groom:

- Have you lost the sacredness of Jesus' birth, death, and resurrection that demonstrate His deep love for you?
- Have you responded to His love by loving others as He loves you?
- Have you made a verbal vow or public statement before other Christians of your covenant with Him?
- Have you circumcised your heart, cutting away your selfishness and self-sufficiency?

- Have you invited and let the gift of the Holy Spirit help you show an accurate replica of Christlike love to others?
- Have you accepted His gracious gift to take your punishment, cover your sin, and offer you eternal life?

Seek Inwardly

Journal your heart to the Lord. Confess where you have taken covenant lightly and not given it the seriousness and sacredness that it deserves. Repent from that perspective and renew your mind to the truth about what the covenant entails. Thank God for the covenant offered to you through Jesus Christ.

Write John 13:34-35 in your journal. Draw a heart around it and ask your Groom to help you love people the way He has loved you.

Seek Outwardly

Think about how you can put John 13:34-35 into practice this week. Be intentional about showing the love of Jesus to others by the way you live.

Day 4: Marriage and Covenant

Try again to get outdoors in God's creation. Ask Him to reveal His presence to you and to teach you more about Him as you spend time with Him.

· · · · · · · · ·

Taking a look back at days 2 and 3, think about how the elements of covenant are part of most weddings. Jesus knew the magnitude of marriage. He knew that God used it as a foreshadowing of Jesus, the Bridegroom, marrying the church, His bride. Marriage in Jesus' day was a very big deal, and everyone knew all of the ceremonial observances that took place. Jesus would use wedding terms to speak with His disciples, because He knew they would understand the reference: He was their Groom and they were His bride, and He was "tying the knot" with them.

Let's look at the elements of a covenant that take place in a wedding ceremony:

Sacredness

The creation of Eve as a helper for Adam was no simple feat. It was a sacred event.

> So the LORD God caused the man to fall into a deep sleep; and while he was sleeping, he took one of the man's ribs and then closed up the place with flesh. Then the LORD God made a woman from the rib he had taken out of the man, and he brought her to the man.
> The man said,
>
> "This is now bone of my bones
>   and flesh of my flesh;
> she shall be called 'woman,'
>   for she was taken out of man."

That is why a man leaves his father and mother and is united to his wife, and they become one flesh. (Genesis 2:21-24)

Adam was speaking covenant language. It was a sacred ceremony initiated by the Creator of the Universe, for the two of them, in front of Him. Symbolic of our covenant with God through Jesus, we are to leave our old life and cleave to Jesus as our Husband. That means "to hold fast and cling together." This is what the phrase "tying the knot" is all about. It's about covenant. When a man and woman stand before God and a group of witnesses in marriage, it is a sacred moment as they reflect on the covenant we have with Jesus Christ.

Sacrifice

The phrase "for better, for worse, in sickness and in health" is commonly used in weddings. Unfortunately, when things get a little rocky in today's marriages, people bail! Making a covenant with another is not for just the good times, but for all times; it will require sacrifice. Often, you must sacrifice your pride. You will have to sacrifice your wants. You may have to choose whether to sacrifice yourself.

Paul said it like this: "Do nothing out of selfish ambition or vain conceit. Rather, in humility value others above yourselves" (Philippians 2:3). The laying down of yourself for another person's needs is symbolic of Jesus' laying His life down for you. He said, "There is no greater love than to lay down one's life for one's friends" (John 15:13, NLT). That is the essence of sacrifice.

Specifics of the Covenant

In the New Testament, when a man wanted to marry a woman, he would go to the father and ask for her hand in marriage. (Many men still do this today.) The father of the bride-to-be would then demand a "bride price," which was usually livestock or grain (much like a dowry).[3] If the groom could meet the father's demands, he would present the gifts. When the bride price was paid, the couple was considered legally married, although they did not live together or consummate the marriage until a year later when their new home was ready.

At salvation, we were betrothed to Jesus. The price for you, His bride, was His life. His great love compelled Him to pay that price for you. He is your Husband, though being with Him in His fullness in heaven does not come right away. And just as we are wed to Christ for eternity, our earthly marriages were intended to be permanent on earth. The phrase "'Til death us do part" is spoken in a marriage ceremony, a promise that you will be husband and wife until you die. It is symbolic of God's promise of eternal life through Jesus for those who belong to Him.

Spoken Vows

At a wedding ceremony, the bride and groom verbally commit them- selves to each other with vows. In Jesus' day, once the two were betrothed, the groom went with his father for a year to build the couple a new home, while the bride stayed in her home preparing herself for the wedding day. Here is the neat part: When the groom left to go build the house with his father, the groom would say, "I go to prepare a place for you; and if I go, I will come again and take you unto myself to be with you always." Sound familiar? It is what Jesus said to His disciples in John 14:2-3. He was talking marriage with them! Jesus spoke His commitment to them (and to us) and will keep every word of it. Ecclesiastes 5:4-5 says, "Fulfill your vow. It is better not to make a vow than to make one and not fulfill it." When you say "I do," you are making a vow before God and many witnesses, just as Jesus spoke covenant with us.

Once the year concluded and the house was built, the groom would call to all of the bride's friends, who were waiting with the oil in their lamps. They would quickly light their lanterns and create a processional, lighting the way for the groom to go to the bride. This is to remind us that Jesus is returning to get His bride.

Showering of Gifts

In Jesus' day, the groom gave the bride a ring made of gold to symbolize purity, and the circle symbolized eternity. These gifts sealed the covenant. Today, when couples get engaged, the groom gives the bride an engagement ring. During the marriage ceremony, they exchange wedding rings. Both of these rings are symbols of the Holy Spirit given to us as a deposit for what is to come, sealing the covenant forever.

At that moment, the bride takes on a new name. She is no longer free to "date" other men. She is her husband's and her husband is hers. The Bible says it like this, "My beloved is mine, and I am his" (Song of Songs 2:16, ESV). This new name identifies her and who she belongs to, giving her a sense of worth and purpose.

Signs

Today, wearing a wedding ring is a sign that you are married. It tells the world that you belong to another. In Jesus' day, another sign of the covenant was a swaddling band, a strip of cloth made by the bride. During the wedding ceremony, the bride's and groom's hands would be wrapped together with the cloth, as a sign of two becoming one. Later on, when they had their first child, the same swaddling band would be used to wrap their child, showing that the child has a mother and father who were committed to each other and to the child.

The best way to show others that we belong to Jesus is love—His love poured out on others because we have been made one with our Groom. Because you have been bound together as one with Christ, through His power within you, you can reproduce more followers of Christ, helping the two of them become wrapped together as one.

Sharing a Meal

Today, most weddings have a rehearsal and then a rehearsal dinner. At this time, the families of the bride and groom come to the same table to eat a meal together, a symbol of covenant.

A day is coming when we will be with our Groom, and we will share a table with Him as a sign of our covenant.

> Let us be glad and rejoice,
>   and let us give honor to him.
> For the time has come for the wedding feast of the Lamb,
>   and his bride has prepared herself. . . .
>
> Blessed are those who are invited to the wedding feast of the Lamb. (Revelation 19:7,9, NLT)

Your loving Groom invites you to His table to eat and be filled.

Wrapping It Up

My hope is that you have seen how the Old Covenant was a foreshadowing of what was to come in the New Covenant through Christ, and that marriage between a man and a woman is to be held as a sacred representation of that covenant. May you know the depth of love that tying the knot with Jesus, your Groom, proves. May it give you a confidence in the love of Jesus like you have never known before.

Loving Response
Seek Upwardly

What has this week's study on covenant meant to you? What have you discovered? How does it make you feel in light of the tremendous seriousness of a covenant? Thank God for His deep love that compelled Him to make this covenant with you.

Seek Inwardly

Journal your heart to God as you contemplate the seriousness, sacredness, deep semblance, and significance of marriage as it relates to the New Covenant in Jesus.

Seek Outwardly

Find a knotted string or rope. Trace the rope or draw one in your journal and write "I Tied the Knot in Covenant with Jesus." Place it in your box to remind you of this incredible gift. You may even want to share with your friends the beauty of covenant relationship with Jesus.

Day 5: Driving Away the Prey

Find another quiet place for you and God out in His creation. Ask Him to speak to you as you complete this week of study.

· · · · · · · · ·

Something in God's covenant with Abraham needs to be highlighted. Once Abraham had killed the animals and presented them as a sacrifice, "Then birds of prey came down on the carcasses, but Abram drove them away" (Genesis 15:11).

Make no mistake about it: Satan does not want you to know the implications of covenant with God. He knows that if you find out everything that covenant means and holds for you, you will be a powerful force as you confidently live a crucified life of love. He feels so threatened by you that he will prey on you in an attempt to disrupt the covenant.

Open your Bible and read 1 Peter 5:8 to discover what this verse says about Satan.

> Be alert and of sober mind. Your enemy the devil prowls around like a roaring lion looking for someone to devour. — 1 Peter 5:8

Satan is a roaring lion seeking whom he may devour. He will do whatever he can to distract you or get you off track from walking with God.

Look at Genesis 15:11 above. Who drove away the birds? Not God, but Abram. Could God have driven away the birds? Absolutely! But He didn't. Consider this: God had already made the promise to Abram, and verse 6 says that Abram believed God. Because he believed God, God could now prepare him for what was to come. Abram had to drive the birds away to set an example to the generations who came behind him. They would go in and take over the land promised them in the covenant, but their enemies were occupying the land. They would have to remember the covenant and drive out their enemies to see the covenant fulfilled. Our loving God is always prepping us for things to come.

Satan will do whatever necessary to detour your focus away from the promises given you through salvation. He doesn't want you to know that you are free from the penalty of sin, that the Holy Spirit will help you live a life of love (see Galatians 5:22), that God's mercy is new every morning (see Lamentations 3:23), that His grace is sufficient (see 2 Corinthians 12:9), that when you are weak, Almighty God is strong, and that you are free to live the abundant life God has for you as you walk with Him (see John 10:10).

Wrapping It Up

The best way to guard against Satan's attacks is to use what God used when He made covenant with Abram: the smoking pot and the flaming torch. Put to death your selfishness and control, and let God's loving presence guide you every step of the way. Stay focused on His promises, for He who promised is faithful (see Hebrews 10:23). Live confidently in His presence. He is your Husband. He will never let those who live in right relationship with Him fall (see Psalm 55:22).

Loving Response

Seek Upwardly

As you discover the truth of who God is as a Promise-Keeper, take your journal and write your response to God. Let the truth that God is a Promise-Keeper sink into the depths of your heart. Pen your thanksgiving to Him.

Seek Inwardly

Reflect on God being a Promise-Keeper. How will this trait of God change the way you think, feel, and act? Record your thoughts and feelings in your journal.

Seek Outwardly

In your journal, record what you will begin doing to show your reciprocated covenant with God. Thank God for the work He is doing in
you as you walk with Him in discovering who He really is.

In your journal, write these words Solomon prayed as he spread
his hands toward heaven: "Lᴏʀᴅ, the God of Israel, there is no God
like you in heaven above or on earth below—you who keep your
covenant of love with your servants who continue wholeheartedly in
your way" (1 Kings 8:23). May you choose to walk wholeheartedly
with God on the path He has set forth for you, crucifying your desires
so that God's perfect love can be displayed in and through you.

Reflect on Jesus' love for you. Your Groom's indescribable love for
you compelled Him to make a personal commitment in covenant
with you. That is both humbling and amazing. Take a piece of rope
and tie it around your wedding finger to remind you of your covenant
with God through Jesus, your Groom.

As you think about what you learned about God this week, try to
capture that in a picture, song lyrics, or art. Bring it, along with your
journal, to your next meeting so you can share all that God is doing
in your heart and life.

the honeymoon is over

Day 1: God Is Not a Genie in a Lamp

If you can, sit outside with the Lord today. Ask Him to reveal Himself to you as you sit in His creation. Don't rush into the study. Be still and quiet and see what He shows you. Then, invite Him to show you more of who He is as you spend this time with Him.

• • • • • • • • •

Over the last three weeks, we have looked at several different views of God. To some, God seems cold and distant, uninvolved and uncaring. To others, God feels like a master manipulator, toying with their emotions and their lives. And some, as we'll learn today, think of God as a genie in a lamp.

Do you remember the scene in Disney's classic movie *Aladdin*? A young peasant finds a discarded old lamp, rubs on it, and out pops a genie, ready to do his new master's bidding. Remember when Aladdin meets the Genie for the first time? Robin Williams is hilarious as he plays the voice of the Genie, laying out the stipulations for getting the three wishes ("and no wishing for more wishes!").

Oftentimes, even without knowing it, we treat God like that. We summon His presence only to make life easy for us. When we need a favor, we "rub His lamp" in prayer and ask Him to help us out by giving us something or getting us out of trouble. When life is going to our satisfaction, we keep God stuffed in the lamp until we need Him again.

Where do we get this mentality? Perhaps from parents who gave us everything we wanted, exactly when we wanted it, and rescued us whenever we got in trouble. Many parents have great intentions to give their kids more than they had. While this is a natural desire, giving children everything can inhibit them from learning how to live responsibly (see Proverbs 19:18-19).

Compounding this problem is American culture, which demands instant gratification instead of discipline, patience, and diligence. Our society has produced generations of people who demand the latest and greatest, the newest and the best, and will go into debt to have it immediately. Microwaves cook in minutes. Internet access is available at lightning speeds, even in the most remote locations. Credit cards allow for maximum pleasure at a minimum cost—until bankruptcy. Broken items—including human beings—are discarded rather than repaired. We live in an egocentric, self-centered, entitled culture.

What does Scripture say about gratification? Read Proverbs 13:12,19 and note what you find.

> Hope deferred makes the heart sick,
>   but a longing fulfilled is a tree of life. . . .
> A longing fulfilled is sweet to the soul,
>   but fools detest turning from evil.
> —Proverbs 13:12,19

The essence of these verses is this: What we long for but have to wait for, we treasure and value more. For example, think about sexual purity. If you long to experience physical intimacy with the guy you love, but have to wait until you are married, you treasure that gift and place a high value on the relationship. If you can, as my parents said, "have the milk without buying the cow," why would the gift of sex within marriage be anything special, sacred, and cherished?

Think about waiting in terms of Christmas: if you give and give and give to your children throughout the year, the gifts given at Christmas are no big deal. But what if children saw something they really wanted and had to wait for it until Christmas morning? That anticipation keeps them up the night before and wakes them up first in the morning to get to the presents. Once they open that gift, they dance around the room, jump up and down, and won't let anybody touch this treasure that they have finally received. It's delayed gratification at its best.

The importance of learning to wait has spiritual implications, too. If you have never learned to wait for something or someone, you may find yourself walking away from your Groom, impatient for eternity. His delay in returning for His bride (you!) may cause you to become disillusioned, discouraged, and untrusting. You may decide that you would be better off controlling your own life since God is so slow in His return and rescue.

Wrapping It Up

You will appreciate and treasure the things for which you learn to wait. Learning delayed gratification means learning to wait on God for answered prayer, rescue, help, and heaven.

Loving Response

Seek Upwardly

As you continue to discover the truth of who God really is, write these words across your journal: "God Is Not a Genie in a Lamp." Then, take a moment to write your thoughts about what you have just learned. Maybe you need to confess that you have felt this way toward

God. Maybe you need to repent of this mindset and invite Him to show you who He really is.

Seek Inwardly
In your journal, write Deuteronomy 32:4:

> He is the Rock, his works are perfect,
>   and all his ways are just.
> A faithful God who does no wrong,
>   upright and just is he.

Express to God that you need His help to trust that His ways are right and good, even when life appears so wrong and so difficult. Ask Him to help you learn to wait with joy, faithfulness, and trust, knowing that His timing is always perfect.

Seek Outwardly
Carry this Scripture verse around with you today and maybe even memorize it. You may just find that you need the reminder, or someone whose path you cross may desperately need to know this truth.

Day 2: God Is a Perfecter

Try to go outside to sit in nature. Look for God to reveal Himself to you. Invite His Spirit to speak to you.

· · · · · · · · ·

I can remember the first few years of my marriage. It was so fun "playing house." Then, out of nowhere bills came. Reality hit! Responsibilities came. Along with them, came conflict. Boy, was I in for a rude awakening! I thought once we got married all problems would end and life would be a bed of roses. The truth was that life was just beginning and God's biggest work was about to be done in my life.

So many people believe that their relationship with Jesus ends when they accept His covenant promise of salvation through faith. Heavens no! That is just the beginning. After you tie the knot with your Groom, you and He begin walking together! He helps you become the person God designed you to be before you were deceived and distracted with sin. Jesus will begin to surface things in your life that are contrary to who He is. He wants to make you holy, the way God created you. It is the only way for you to be happy, fulfilled, and free. But be certain of this: It takes time and patience from both Him and you.

Open your Bible and read James 1:2-4 to discover what Scripture says about perfecting you. Write down your thoughts in your journal.

> Consider it pure joy, my brothers and sisters, whenever you face trials of many kinds, because you know that the testing of your faith produces perseverance. Let perseverance finish its work so that you may be mature and complete, not lacking anything. —James 1:2-4

Be happy when troubles and struggles come into my life? That's crazy! And yet, James told us that through those troubles and

Maturing Us!

struggles, God does His greatest work in our lives to make us perfect. Now, before you get concerned about this word *perfect*, let me explain what it really means. It does *not* mean to be free of flaws or defects. This word literally means "matured" and is used in the context of farming. A farmer must plant seeds in prepared soil. The seed must endure heat from the sun and rain from the storms, yet both are essential to the process of growing the seed. The seed is perfect, or mature, when it is ripe, fully developed, and ready to be used (eaten!).

God wants you to be fully developed and ripened, becoming who He designed you to be. He wants others to see who God really is from the fruit in your life. He wants your life to bring Him glory. Living in this surrendered state before Him takes a whole lot of patience and trust in your Groom as He walks with you through the heat and the storms.

So how do we stay in this with our Groom and not get frustrated, impatient, and hopeless? What do we do when we feel as if the honeymoon is over? Jesus gave us some great encouragement. Read John 15:1-8. Record in your journal what you learn from these verses.

I am the true vine, and my Father is the gardener. He cuts off every branch in me that bears no fruit, while every branch that does bear fruit he prunes so that it will be even more fruitful. You are already clean because of the word I have spoken to you. Remain in me, as I also remain in you. No branch can bear fruit by itself; it must remain in the vine. Neither can you bear fruit unless you remain in me.

I am the vine; you are the branches. If you remain in me and I in you, you will bear much fruit; apart from me you can do nothing. If you do not remain in me, you are like a branch that is thrown away and withers; such branches are picked up, thrown into the fire and burned. If you remain in me and my words remain in you, ask whatever you wish, and it will be done for you. This is to my Father's glory, that you bear much fruit, showing yourselves to be my disciples. — John 15:1-8

In some Bible translations the word *remain* is "abide," but both have a very common meaning. To remain or abide with Jesus means to be rooted in Him, knit together with Him as He makes Himself at home in your heart. It means to allow Him access to every single part of your life, holding nothing back from Him, fully permitting and inviting Him into every decision and every activity. Just as a branch cannot survive without staying attached to the Vine, all nourishment—all growth, understanding, discernment, strength, and hope—comes from Him. This requires a constant connection and deep communication as bride and Groom.

Wrapping It Up

Abundant life begins when you get saved, making covenant with Jesus. As you begin walking with God, He begins to perfect you. You can partner with Him in this process by staying close to Him, like a branch remains in the Vine.

Loving Response

Seek Upwardly

Thank God for His willingness to walk with you and make you all that He intends for you to be. Grab an unripened banana. The banana is to serve as a reminder of what happens when we remain with our Groom through all the seasons of life, even troubles and struggles. We may feel as though the honeymoon is over, but your Groom is showing you an even greater depth of His love.

Seek Inwardly

Journal about the process you have observed of a banana going from unripened to fully ripened and ready for use. Talk with God about His being your Perfecter. Then record John 15:5,8 in your journal. Tell Him that you will surrender to the process of maturing and helping you regain what was lost by sin, getting you back to the way God created you.

Seek Outwardly

Write "God Is a Perfecter" on a piece of paper and stick it in your box to remind you of this truth during the week. Every time you attach your cell phone to its charger, remind yourself that you must stay attached to the Vine for your perfecting to take place. Share this with a friend who may need to hear this truth.

Day 3: Quick-Fix Temptations

As you sit out in nature today, ask your Father to declare who He is through what He has created, and to speak to you as you spend this time with Him.

. . . .

"You've got problems? We've got solutions!" This is the marketing strategy of every product on the market. If there is a common problem, and you can find a solution, you have got a great product that will sell to a lot of people, because people are always looking for answers!

In addition to our Husband allowing tough times to grow and ripen us, we face an enemy who works against the process, trying to lure us away from Jesus to follow our own desires. He is the master marketer, trying to deceive you into thinking that you've got problems but he has the answers that will offer you a quick fix. While God certainly tests and proves us to help us become like Him, He does not tempt and entice us to do evil. Satan is the one who entices and deceives us into sin and thus seeks to separate us from the Father. Then, when we are struggling, he tries to deceive us and draw us away even more.

Isn't that exactly what happened to Adam and Eve? They were walking with God in the Garden of Eden, and Satan came and tempted the woman. He appealed to her fleshly desires and made evil look good and good look evil. This distortion of the truth caused Eve to doubt God's goodness. She was deceived by lies, chose disobedience, and headed down the road of destruction. It's been going on just like this ever since. Can you relate?

Satan is cunning, sowing seeds of doubt at the core of your being: your beliefs. If he can make you doubt God's goodness, he's got his hook in you to deceive and destroy you.

Read Genesis 3:1-5 carefully. In your journal, record how Satan sowed doubt in Eve's belief system.

> Now the serpent was more crafty than any of the wild animals the LORD God had made. He said to the woman, "Did God really say, 'You must not eat from any tree in the garden'?"
>
> The woman said to the serpent, "We may eat fruit from the trees in the garden, but God did say, 'You must not eat fruit from the tree that is in the middle of the garden, and you must not touch it, or you will die.'"
>
> "You will not certainly die," the serpent said to the woman. "For God knows that when you eat from it your eyes will be opened, and you will be like God, knowing good and evil." —Genesis 3:1-5

ask for wisdom!

When he approached Eve in the garden, his first question was, "Did God really say, 'You must not eat from any tree in the garden?'" (Genesis 3:1). Satan always begins with doubt. Then, he continued with half-truths (deception): "You will not certainly die! . . . For God knows that when you eat from it your eyes will be opened, and you will be like God, knowing good and evil" (Genesis 3:4-5). As a result, "When the woman saw [or was convinced] that the fruit of the tree was good for food and pleasing to the eye [or appealing to her senses], and also desirable for gaining wisdom [or appealing to her desires], she took some and ate it." Satan lured her into disobedience, enticing her to trust in herself and his lies instead of God's truth.

accept God's word!

James said it like this: "But each person is tempted when they are dragged away by their own evil desire and enticed. Then, after desire has conceived, it gives birth to sin; and sin, when it is full-grown, gives birth to death" (James 1:14-15). Seeds of God's truth lead to life and maturity. Seeds of evil lead to death and destruction.

Here's the good news: God has made a way for His bride to overcome temptation so that we can continue to grow with Him. In 1 Corinthians 10:13, Paul wrote, "No temptation has overtaken you except what is common to mankind. And God is faithful; he will not let you be tempted beyond what you can bear. But when you are tempted, he will also provide a way out so that you can endure it."

So the question then becomes, "How do I escape Satan's attempts to get me to disobey and thus lose my connection with my Groom, as He seeks to help me grow?" We start with the source: our belief system, our doubting. James said in James 1:5-8 that if you lack wisdom, God will generously give it to you but you have to ask in faith, with no doubting. He goes on to say that if you doubt, you are like the waves of the sea, driven by the wind and tossed; and that you shouldn't think that you will receive anything from the Lord because you are double-minded (saying you trust God and yet doubting) and unstable in all your ways (one minute moving forward with God and the next going in the opposite direction). So the first way of escape is to ask God for wisdom. Ask Him to show you where the enemy is seeking to make you doubt and to reveal the way to escape. Then, you must fully trust, without a doubt, that He will give it to you.

James went on to say, "Humbly accept the word planted in you, which can save you. Do not merely listen to the word, and so deceive yourselves. Do what it says" (1:21-22). The person who "continues in it — not forgetting what they have heard, but doing it — they will be blessed in what they do" (1:25). Thus, our second way of escape is to accept God's Word as concrete truth and live accordingly. Obeying God's Word as you keep it before you will guard against your going astray. God's presence will be with you and you can continue to move forward with Him as your Perfecter.

Wrapping It Up

Here it is in a nutshell: When Satan tries to drag you away from God's presence and His perfecting of you, ask God to help you see the deception for what it is and respond appropriately. Begin to focus on who God is: Present, Pursuing, a Promise-Keeper, and a Perfecter. And don't just know it in your head, but be convinced of it in the depths of your heart. Let who He is captivate your mind so much that it changes the way you live, proving that you confidently believe it to be true. You declare, "God is with me, calling me to walk with Him as His very own. He is so committed to me that He is using all things, even this temptation, to mature me." This declaration causes Satan to flee because you resisted Him (see James 4:7) and his mind game did not work on you!

As a result, you are promised that your joy will grow as you continue to walk with God, because He is restoring you to the way He made you to live: happy, fulfilled, and free! This enables you to stand up under Satan's attacks, because his attempts to make you doubt don't faze you anymore! You know your Groom, and nobody can change your mind!

Loving Response

Seek Upwardly

Can you relate to Satan's attempts to lure you away from walking with your perfecting Husband? Can you attest that Satan often causes you to doubt God's goodness? Take some time to write in your journal, talking with God about what you have learned. Confess and repent, and ask God to help you move forward with Him, overcoming the enemy's attempts to lure you away. There's nothing He would rather do!

Seek Inwardly

Think about this for a minute: What would happen if you had started out with just a banana plant and had put it in your box, shutting it up tightly and taping it down on all sides? It would not have grown but rather dried up or died altogether. God wants to ripen you. Satan wants to destroy you.

Satan is the true game-player! Choose today to no longer allow the enemy to shut up your growth with your Protecter. Be intentional about knowing Your Husband in the very depths of your heart and walking with Him in His presence with confidence.

Seek Outwardly

Be encouraged with this incredible promise: "The Lord knows how to rescue the godly from temptation" (2 Peter 2:9, NASB). Write this verse in your journal and thank your Groom for rescuing you from temptation. Share this verse as an encouragement to those around you who are struggling with the temptations of the evil one.

Day 4: The Justice of God

Try to sit outside again today or get near a window. Take in all the love gifts that God gives you as He is present with you, using His creation to further pursue you.

· · · · · · · · ·

"God, what are you doing?" Ever asked that one? I know I have!

Satan is so relentless in making us question God's goodness that when God is just, we begin to question how a loving and good God can also be so harsh in His justice. If God is so good, why would He let people go to hell? Better yet, if God is so good, why would He allow bad things to happen to His bride? Where is this Groom I fell in love with, whom I now call Husband? Where is His deep, unconditional, unfathomable, indescribable love for me now? If we begin to question God's goodness, we can begin to question if He truly does love us and will either jump into performance mode to please Him and win back His love or quit and walk away, believing that the honeymoon is over.

But God is love. And God is good. And God is just. These are not virtues that God has developed over eternity; they are who He is. He cannot separate Himself from various virtues at various times. If they were only character attributes, then they could be minimized, maximized, or go away all together. But because they are who He is, they will always exist and they will always be in harmony with one another. Because we hold virtues that can be minimized, maximized, or changed, we think God is the same. But we cannot make God into a human being.

If I were mixing up cake batter, I would mix various ingredients together. But once that batter is mixed, it is just called "batter," not all the ingredients. There is no way of separating them out. They are all considered the batter. They don't conflict with one another or contradict one another; they are one. They just "are."

In the same way, the many facets of God are all one. Why is this important to remember? Because if you begin to believe that they can be separated out independent of each other, then you will try to apply one without the other and will distort who God really is. You might even blame Him and get angry at Him for something He didn't do.

So how do God's goodness and His justice work together?

God created us in His image and likeness, and desired that we would lead the world with His heart under the guidelines of morality set forth in His Word. These guidelines were not intended to punish us or withhold good from us, because God is good. He wants us to be the happiest people on the planet! "If you, then, though you are evil, know how to give good gifts to your children, how much more will your Father in heaven give good gifts to those who ask him!" (Matthew 7:11).

God gave moral (meaning "a standard of behavior and character") guidelines as a way of protection, to keep us from being hurt. When my children were little, I would tell them that they could go anywhere in the yard but not to go into the street. Did I set that standard because I was mean and simply liked to withhold good from my children? Absolutely not! I want the best for my children because I desperately love them, so I set the boundary to protect them! So it is with God.

Just as I confronted my children when they overstepped the boundary and went out in the street, our loving Husband confronts us when we step out from under His moral guidelines, which we have all done. "For all have sinned and fall short of the glory of God" (Romans 3:23). We have *all* stepped out from under God's moral guidelines. In His justice (judging whether we have stayed within the guidelines or not, and determining if we get reward or punishment accordingly), He sentences us. And because we have all sinned, we are all under the sentence of death. This does not sound like love, or goodness, but it is the most loving thing He could do!

He loved us enough to place on us His guidelines of protection. He loved us enough to allow justice to fall upon us for choosing to step away from His guidelines. But He also loved us enough to apply mercy and grace should we choose to accept the blood of His everlasting covenant through the death of His Son, Jesus. This is how He can be loving, just, and good all at the same time.

When God looks at a sinner who has accepted Christ, He doesn't see him the same way He sees someone who is continually overstepping His guidelines. When God looks at a sinner who continues to love sin, His justice sentences him to death. When God looks at a sinner who accepts Jesus' payment for his sin and gets back within the moral guidelines set for him, God's justice sentences him to life. And God is just in both of these. Love, goodness, mercy, and grace couldn't be loving, good, merciful, and gracious without justice. If God chose who would go to heaven or hell randomly, that would not be fair. And if God isn't fair, then He isn't loving. He certainly cannot be merciful and gracious when He is picking and choosing randomly who enters heaven and who does not.

Wrapping It Up

God's love compels the moral guidelines. His love allows you to choose to love Him in return, or to reject His Son. While He desires you to stay within the moral guideleines of protection set before you in His Word, He will not force you. He wants you to choose to love Him and obey Him. In response, His love offers fair justice based on your choices.

Loving Response

Seek Upwardly

Across your journal today, write "God Is Good." If He were not good, He would not be just, because His justice is right and fair. My heart for you today is to be convinced that your Husband is good. Thank Him for His love that compels both His goodness and His justice when we choose to go our own way instead of trusting in His loving guidelines and walking in obedience.

Seek Inwardly

Talk with God about your struggles with His goodness and His justice. Do you love and adore God when He is good, but when He is just (which we bring upon ourselves and yet blame God when He responds), you reject Him? Why? What is that about? How do I overcome that belief system?

Seek Outwardly

Record these words from Psalm 136:1: "Give thanks to the LORD, for he is good." Try to memorize this verse today. As you go throughout this day, make your response, "God is good" no matter what the circumstance, good or bad. This declaration of trust will draw you back into the loving presence of your Groom and give you the confidence to face anything this day may bring. Take this truth with you today for yourself and possibly for another who will cross your path, someone who may desperately need to hear this truth.

Day 5: Omniscient

Go out in nature today and ask God to make Himself obvious to you through all that He has made.

· · · · · · · · ·

Have you ever seen the movie *Vantage Point*? Several different people see a crime from different vantage points and their points give the clues necessary to solve the crime. When it comes to God, we need to remember that even though we may have our vantage point of our circumstances in life, He has the ultimate vantage point that we can't see.

Our Husband is not a genie in a lamp, existing only to make life easy for you. He is a jealous Husband who wants your total devotion and will stop at nothing to have your heart completely. He wants you to live the abundant life He created you to have, and knows just what you need to get to that place. He knows how to prepare you to experience all He has for you. As His bride, you have to trust that He is good, even when the hard times come, even when Satan seeks to make you doubt.

Even though He is the Perfecter, what we may see as bad from our perspective might truly be good from His vantage point. God often allows "bad" things to happen that turn out to be the best thing. Moses had to run for his life for murdering someone. We see that as a terrible series of events. God saw it as good. If Moses hadn't run into the wilderness, he may have missed God's call (through the burning bush) to go save His bride. Joseph was sold into slavery by his brothers. Joseph probably saw that as bad. God saw it as good because He knew that a famine would occur and His bride would need to get help from Egypt, which is where Joseph ended up as the second in command (see Genesis 42–50).

A multimillionaire makes a bad business decision and loses everything. We see it as bad. God sees it as good. God knew that if he kept up this pace, he would become a workaholic and miss out on raising his four sons. Losing it all makes him become an excellent father as he learns that people are more important than money.

A married woman is hurrying down the road and her car breaks down. When she jumps out to see what happened, she is hit by oncoming traffic and wakes up in the emergency room. We see that as bad. God sees that as good, because He knew that she was headed to have an affair with a married man and devastate two families had her car not broken down. These seemingly bad circumstances are really demonstrations of God's grace.

Read Isaiah 55:8-9 and record what we must constantly keep in mind.

> "For my thoughts are not your thoughts,
>   neither are your ways my ways,"
>   declares the LORD.
> "As the heavens are higher than the earth,
>   so are my ways higher than your ways
>   and my thoughts than your thoughts."
> —Isaiah 55:8-9

God is omniscient. He knows everything. Absolutely everything. He knows where you are and what lies ahead. He will use seemingly bad things to save and mature you, His bride. He will do whatever He has to do to turn your heart toward Him. He also knows what His bride needs, and may even allow you to go through something so that you can help others.

A woman divorces her husband and then remarries him, and out of that pain a marriage ministry is birthed. A lady aborts her baby, and out of that pain births a ministry to pregnant women. A young lady is diagnosed with cancer and out of her trips to the hospital for chemotherapy, several other ladies come to know Jesus as Lord and Savior. These three women would all say that their greatest misery has become their greatest ministry. Their ministries are purely a gift of God's grace.

As a murderer, did Moses deserve to lead God's people out of slavery in Egypt? God's justice might say no. But God's mercy said yes. Mercy triumphed because Moses was humbled and surrendered at the burning bush. Had Moses not had a humble heart, God's justice may have won and things would have looked much different. God's mercy has been working throughout your whole life. Otherwise, the first time you sinned, God's justice would have pronounced death on you and you would have immediately died. God's mercy has put a hold on God's justice because He is not willing for any to perish (see 2 Peter 3:9). God's mercy is always at work, as are His grace and His justice. The outcome of your life is based on your perspective and response to His mercy, grace, and justice at work in your life.

God is good at all times for all time. He can be trusted to use all things to mature you. Your Husband loves you enough to allow you to go through difficulties to help you return to the original way He created you to be happy, fulfilled, and free. But should you choose to doubt His goodness and His love, His justice will allow you to suffer the consequences of your choices, even if they are painful. However, in the midst of that pain, if you choose to humble yourself and surrender, your Husband's mercy will hold off justice, allowing God's grace to use your pain to benefit yourself and others.

Wrapping It Up

God is good. Even when you feel that the honeymoon is over, His heart toward you is good. He is omniscient and sees from a vantage point that you do not. He has your best interest at heart. He can be trusted. His goodness works all things together for your good (see Romans 8:28) and for your maturity. Why? Because He is your Husband and wants you to be all that you were intended to be. He loves you that much.

Loving Response

Seek Upwardly

As you understand the true definition of God as a present God who pursues you in relationship, who becomes your Husband as a Promise-Keeper, and who perfects you as you walk together, be confident that the intent of your loving Husband is good. Your Perfecter loves you and wants the best for you, whether it feels or looks like it or not. Out of deep love and a desire for you to fulfill the purposes for which He made you, He allows troubles in your life. His omniscience knows what you need. Trust Him, trust Him, trust Him.

Seek Inwardly

Think about the implications of God as Perfecter. How will that character trait change the way you think, feel, and act? How will it change the way you look at life? Write your thoughts in your journal. Thank God for the work He is doing in you as you walk with Him in discovering who He really is.

Seek Outwardly

Write Proverbs 3:5-6 in your journal. Try to memorize this verse today. Talk with God about how He relates to you and how you have misunderstood His heart toward you. Confess the times when you have questioned His goodness toward you and thus have questioned His love for you. If you were married and your husband questioned your heart like you question His, how would it make you feel? God does love you deeply and longs for you to know the depth of that love, that He is fully committed to you.

Under the verse, write: "I Trust You; It's All Good." You may also want to simply write this on the palm of your hand or on your forearm to remind you of this throughout your day. God is good, and He can be trusted at all times.

Think about what you learned about who God is this week. Seek to capture that in a picture, song lyrics, or art. Bring your work and your journal with you to your next group meeting so you can share all that God is doing in your heart and life.

my better half

Day 1: God Is Not a Parole Officer

God's character shows up in all that He created. Sit with Him each day this week and ask Him to reveal Himself to you. Write down what He shows you so you won't forget and so you can share it with your group and encourage each other. You will be amazed at what He shows you!

· · · · · · · · ·

Tattletale! Did someone ever call you that? Did you ever call someone else that? As a child, there always seemed to be someone right there to catch me whenever I did the wrong thing. They always thought it their responsibility to tell the authorities on me. It felt like a policeman was always looking over my shoulder, waiting to blow the whistle.

For some, growing up in a family was more like a prison than a home. Perhaps your parents had rules that you were expected to obey, and there was neither discussion nor openness to share your heart or feelings. Or perhaps your parents responded very harshly if you did not walk the "straight and narrow," so you lived life simply waiting for the next hammer to fall. Maybe fear of making one false move or being in trouble paralyzed you, keeping you constantly tense and walking on eggshells. That fear may have propelled you to appease your parents in order to avoid their wrath. As a result, you stuffed your heart deep within, choosing not to feel and doing your best to stay under the radar of their wrath.

Can you think of the ramifications of someone who lives like this and then projects that parent image onto God? Even those who have walked with God for a long time still live under the idea of a tyrant god. This god is like a parole officer, whose only job is to make sure you stay in line and don't screw up; the moment you do, his punishment is quick and harsh, doled out to get you back in line.

God is not a parole officer, watching your every move or waiting for the chance to punish you. God is not filled with rage and hatred; you do not have to appease Him, trying to get Him to like you to avoid His wrath. You don't have to "calm God down."

Yes, God is to be feared. Yes, God does discipline us. But God takes no pleasure in your pain.

When I was growing up, I adored my mother. I still do. She showed me Jesus with skin on every day of my life. She was not perfect, but she showed me unconditional love, servanthood, selflessness, sacrifice, and so much more. I also knew what my mother expected of me, and what would happen if I didn't follow her instructions: I got a whippin'. And that spanking would be a doozie, so that I would never even consider making that poor choice ever again! I knew my mother loved me deeply, but I also knew that if I disobeyed her, she would discipline me. Because of this dual role that she played, I held an indescribable and incredible respect for her. This is healthy fear.

Throughout biblical history, people held high respect for their king. They bowed to his authority. They recognized that he held the power to protect and provide, but he also held the power to put an end to them all. Again, healthy fear.

In the movie *The Lion King* every time Mufasa's name was spoken, the hyenas would shudder and say, "Ooooooo, Mufasa!" showing deep reverence for both his position of authority and his power granted to do whatever he wished to whomever he wished.

These three examples best describe the fear of the Lord from a human standpoint. It's the understanding that there is a God who is deeply in love with you, who out of His love and goodness will allow His justice to respond to your willful disobedience in order to perfect you. Yet even in His justice, His mercy is long-suffering with you and His grace is always available to those who will humble themselves and return to His love, where real life abides.

Read Proverbs 19:23, and record what a healthy fear of the Lord promotes.

> The fear of the LORD leads to life;
>   then one rests content, untouched by trouble.
> —Proverbs 19:23

Wrapping It Up

The older I've gotten, and having become a mother myself, I now understand all those times when my mother would say, "This hurts me more than it hurts you" or "This is because I love you," when she punished me. How true those statements really were. Just like my mother hated to punish me, she knew it was for my good. Your Husband is the same way. He allows you to choose to obey or disobey and suffer the consequences of your choices. Though it pains Him to do so, He knows it is for your benefit. He truly is your better half.

Loving Response

Seek Upwardly

In your journal, draw a picture that symbolizes a parole officer to you. Put a huge X over it, and write beside or below it, "God Is Not a Parole Officer." Dialogue with your Husband about a healthy fear of Him, not as a parole officer, but as a Lover to be revered. In your journal, record what He tells you. Confess when you have felt this way about Him. Turn away from that mentality and ask Him to show you His true identity consumed solely in love.

Seek Inwardly

Have you treated God like He is your parole officer? Have you blamed God for your bad choices? Have you become embittered toward God because you didn't get your way? How might you need to humble yourself and turn from this wrong perspective?

Seek Outwardly

In your journal, write Proverbs 1:7: "The fear of the LORD is the beginning of knowledge." This was the first phrase King Solomon wrote in the Book of Proverbs. When God told Solomon to ask whatever he wanted and He would give it to him, King Solomon asked for wisdom (see 1 Kings 3:4-9). King Solomon understood the correct meaning of the fear of the Lord and thus knew that the best thing to ask for was to know God's depth of love, but also His unlimited power to shut down even the most powerful man on earth. Solomon understood that the fear of the Lord was truly the most important thing to possess. King Solomon held deep reverence for His God because He understood the fear of the Lord.

Day 2: God Is Your Partner

Try to get outside to sit in nature and look for God to reveal Himself to you. Be reminded that God is present with you even now and longs to reveal Himself more and more to you. Invite His Spirit to guide you into His truth.

• • • • • • • • •

Because God is always present, you are never alone. He is constantly pursuing you so He can show you His love. At salvation, we, His bride, make covenant with Him, our Groom, and He holds true to His covenant forever. He walks with you and shows you areas in your life that need to be removed and replaced with His likeness. In order to do that, He sometimes allows troubles and pain to show you your sin. When you refuse to repent, He lets you live with your choices. It is as if He is saying, "Okay, if you think you know better, then have at it, but I will be here waiting on you when you are ready to return to Me and trust Me." It is the heart of God to partner with you and help you return to the way He originally created you to be: happy, fulfilled, and free. But you must allow Him to partner with you.

God partners with you by offering you precepts, principles, and promises.

A **precept** of God is a command of God concerning how you are to conduct yourself with Him and with others. The Ten Commandments (see Exodus 20) are precepts of God. The Great Commandment (see Matthew 22:36-40) to love the Lord with all of who you are and to love your neighbor as yourself is a precept, a command of God that sums up and supports the Ten Commandments. The Great Commission (see Matthew 28:18-20) is a precept, a command of God to invite others to live under The Great Commandment. If something is written in Scripture as an imperative, requiring your immediate action, it is a precept. These precepts are not suggestions; they are commands of God. They are the guidelines that God created for your protection that include both what to do and what *not* to do. Precepts refer to your actions.

A **principle** of God may not be written as a precept or command, but following and obeying God's principles is implied. For example, the Bible does not explicitly say, "don't physically wound another person" or "don't maim another person." But a principle throughout Scripture is to put others ahead of yourself (see Philippians 2:3), to think of others before yourself (see Romans 12:10), and to treat others with kindness and respect (see Ephesians 4:32). Couple those precepts with the command of God, "You shall not murder" (Exodus 20:13), and I think we understand God's heart about hurting and maiming others without a specific command being stated in Scripture. Principles are focused more on your heart than on your actions. Principles support the commands, but God is more interested in your understanding His heart and your responding out of your heart than responding to rules without your heart's involvement.

However, oftentimes we as Christians look for "biblical loopholes" that let us get by with bad behavior, because God didn't specifically address a particular issue. In our search to find the loopholes, we miss God's heart. For example, imagine that a man mutilated and permanently disfigured another man over a girlfriend. His defense is, "Well, the Bible doesn't say you can't mutilate or disfigure; it just says don't murder, and I didn't murder." Would that defense fly? Would we say, "Well, you have a point. Let's let him go free without penalty"? Absolutely not! We would all say that the Bible doesn't say anything against disfiguring another person but it certainly is implied; not maiming someone is a given. This is a principle, not intended to be ignored or watered down. We may think my example is ridiculous, but the sad thing is that many people—even Christians—look for and live by the loopholes they create all the time.

I was asked to speak to a group of high school students about what God says regarding abstinence. I began to share God's precept "Do not commit adultery," His principles that show His heart behind that precept, and the promises that are offered for those who wait in obedience to His command. As the leader opened the floor for questions, one girl said, "God said don't commit adultery. That is for married people, telling them not to have an affair, right?" My answer was that God's definition of adultery is sex outside of marriage, and given the correct definition, sex before marriage is outside of marriage and thus is something God forbids. Another person raised this question: "Well, the Bible only says not to have sex outside of marriage, but everything else is okay, since it is not intercourse, right?" My answer was that God's definition of sex is anything that causes sexual urges to be gratified, and though not explicitly stated, other activities were certainly implied.

I went on to say that when God said, "Do not murder," we would not say, "I can slice someone up, maim him, cut each finger off one at a time, and make him suffer tremendous pain, because God only said that I can't murder someone." Or let's say that I ran to the store and told my children not to eat the cookies while I was gone because it would ruin their supper. Instead they ate cake, claiming that I didn't forbid that dessert. My children got the precept but did not get my heart, the principle. I implied not to ruin dinner by eating dessert first, but because I didn't actually say it, they felt justified. These are the games we play with God's Word, missing God's heart behind His precepts. God is omniscient. He knows your heart. He knows when you are trying to get away with sin by finding loopholes in His Word.

Finally, God gives us His **promises**. Promises of God are not blatant commands or implied commands of God, but are rather commitments that He makes and guarantees. He provides promises to encourage you as you seek to live out His commands, so that you can be perfected.

Open your Bible and read 2 Peter 1:4. Summarize it in your own words.

> He has given us his very great and precious promises, so that through them you may participate in the divine nature, having escaped the corruption in the world caused by evil desires. — 2 Peter 1:4

God promises to never leave you nor forsake you (see Deuteronomy 31:6). He promises that He will repay those who harm you (see Romans 12:19). He promises to supply your every need (see Philippians 4:19). He promises to give you strength when you are weak (see Isaiah 40:31). He promises to give you everything you ask for in His name (see John 14:13).

Your Husband wants to **partner** with you to perfect you by offering you His precepts, principles, and promises.

Read Matthew 11:28-30 and write how this partnership works.

> Come to me, all you who are weary and burdened, and I will give you rest. Take my yoke upon you and learn from me, for I am gentle and humble in heart, and you will find rest for your souls. For my yoke is easy and my burden is light. — Matthew 11:28-30

In Jesus' day, a yoke was a rabbi's interpretation of how to apply the Scriptures in everyday life. The word *rest* meant "peace for the journey ahead."

Wrapping It Up

Jesus says to you, "Take on my precepts and my heart behind my principles and let me perfect you; I want to help you and I will not be forceful or demanding, but rather patient and supportive as you grow and learn. In this, your mind and heart will be at peace as we walk this journey together, because you are not alone." Your Husband truly is the better half.

Loving Response

Seek Upwardly

Oh, that you would see the tremendous love your Husband has for you! He didn't say, "Live like Me" and leave you on your own to hope for the best. He said, "Live like Me, and here's a book that I inspired to help you know what that looks like." What a sad day it will be for those who have ignored His Word and walked in disobedience. For when they say, "I didn't know what to do!" God will respond, "But I wrote it down for you!"

Seek Inwardly

In your journal, write down your thoughts and feelings as you have met with your Husband today. Let Him convict where needed, encourage where needed, and affirm where needed. Offer thanksgiving to Him for giving you His precepts that protect and not punish, His principles that show you His heart, and His promises that help you move forward in growth. Thank Him for not leaving you to figure it out on your own, but for being your partner to perfect you.

Seek Outwardly

In your journal, write down the great promises listed above, along with others that the Spirit brings to your mind. Then write this Scripture verse from 2 Chronicles 6:10, "The LORD has kept the promise he made." Thank your Husband for keeping His promises, and for giving you the confidence that He can be relied and counted on.

Write "God Is Your Partner" on a piece of paper and stick it in your box to remind you of this truth during the week.

Day 3: The Alongsider

As you sit out in nature today, ask your Father to declare to you who He is through what He created, and to speak to you as you spend this time with Immanuel, the with-us God.

• • • • • • • • •

Oftentimes, I run alone. But truthfully, I push myself much harder when I run with my husband. When I start lagging behind, stop to walk, or huff, puff, and grunt, Dale begins to encourage me, challenge me, and inspire me to finish strong. God gave us the Holy Spirit to do the same as we run this race of life.

Not only did your Husband give you precepts, principles, and promises to partner with you in your perfection, but He gave you a *Paraclete*—the promised Holy Spirit to help you.

Read John 14:16-17, and note what it says about the Holy Spirit.

> And I will ask the Father, and he will give you another advocate to help you and be with you forever—the Spirit of truth.—John 14:16-17

In this verse, the word *advocate* is *parakletos* and means "to come alongside to help; a consoler; an advocate." Your Husband is so committed to your maturity and happiness that He gave you the Holy Spirit to come alongside you to console you. That means to give you emotional support. Have you ever felt so down or tired or weak or insecure and then experienced the Holy Spirit reminding you who you are and whose you are? It truly is amazing! Your Husband has given you the Spirit for emotional support when you need Him. He is always in your corner, always fighting for you and cheering you on.

Jesus went on to say, "But the Advocate, the Holy Spirit, whom the Father will send in my name, will teach you all things and will remind you of everything I have said to you" (John 14:26). Picture your Husband not sending you flowers with a love note attached, but rather sending you His Spirit with a love note attached. His Spirit will show you more of who He is and help you remember everything that He has told you.

It reminds me of a soldier going off to war, leaving a video saved on the family computer, filled with everything he wants his loved ones to know. He leaves it so they can hear his voice and play it over and over again, never forgetting his love and devotion to them. The great love of your Husband has done this for you, so that you would not feel alone in this journey toward maturity.

Finally, Jesus also said, "But when he, the Spirit of truth, comes, he will guide you into all the truth" (John 16:13). A guide is someone who shows the way, especially when new territory lies ahead. New territory comes after your covenant is made with your Husband. You are now learning how to walk with Him, hear His voice, and live in obedience to His precepts. That's new! And you need someone to help guide you. This is what the Holy Spirit does. The Holy Spirit can speak to you, and you can hear Him. How else would He console you, cheer you on, teach you, remind you, and guide you?

As you read your Bible, the Spirit will lead you to pause on one verse that consoles, cheers, teaches, reminds, or guides you. It may be a verse that you have never understood before, and He gives you complete clarity about it. The Holy Spirit may speak through people. And as I hope you have experienced while sitting outside, He speaks through His creation. Just know that you can also hear the voice of the Spirit speaking directly to you.

The other morning, I woke up to have my morning jog and a song was already playing in my head. I said, "Good morning, Jesus! Is this the artist that You want me to listen to while I run today?" I heard Him say, "Yes." I asked Him, "Is that a yes?" and He said, "Yes." I found that particular artist on my iPhone and the music so ministered to me; it was just what I needed for that day. That was my Husband's way of saying, "I love you."

On a flight to Montana, I read a great book. When I arrived, I only had two chapters left, so I thought that I could just read them on the flight home. I laid the book with my Bible where I sat to have my time with my Husband each day. A dear friend came over to visit. I went outside to play with her children while she stayed inside with her baby. After a little time, they went home. On the morning of my flight home, I was brushing my teeth and the Spirit told me to give my friend my book. I argued with God that I only had two chapters left (like He didn't know). I even found myself bargaining with God that if He would let me keep it, I would buy her a new one and mail it to her so it wouldn't have all my writing in it. But the Spirit kept telling me to give her the book. When she came to tell me goodbye, I reluctantly said, "God told me to give you this." My friend burst into tears and explained, "Yesterday as I sat here with the baby, I noticed your book. I looked at the title. It spoke to where I am and what I need to hear from the Father. I picked it up, held it to my chest and said, 'Oh God, I want to live this close to You. I want desperately to know You like this book title says. Lord, I need this book.'" I had no idea she had done that, but God did; He told me to offer a love gift to my friend, who is also His bride.

Wrapping It Up

Your Husband wants you to be all that God created you to be, even more than you do! He has committed Himself to you by not only giving you the way to live (the Bible), but then giving you a Helper, the Holy Spirit, to speak to you, console you, cheer you on, teach you, remind you, and guide you. You really can run this race of life, because you have the perfect Alongsider cheering you on!

Loving Response

Seek Upwardly

In a few places, the Bible tells us not to quench the Spirit and not to grieve the Spirit (see 1 Thessalonians 5:19; Ephesians 4:30). To quench the Spirit means that when He speaks to you, you just ignore Him or are closed to Him, like putting out a spark before it becomes a fire. To grieve the Spirit means for you to do the opposite of how He directs, like putting to death His counsel. That grieves the Holy Spirit.

Find some matches around the house. Strike one match and let it burn until it almost reaches your fingers. Let that image serve as a reminder to listen and respond to the Holy Spirit, rather than putting out His flaming words and walking in disobedience. Place the matches in your box to remind you that the Holy Spirit wants to speak to you if you will listen.

Seek Inwardly
Tape the match you burned into your journal. Think about the times you may have quenched or grieved His Spirit. Confess that to God and ask His forgiveness. Ask Him to speak to you again because you want to listen this time and follow His leading. If you have never heard God speak before, ask Him to allow you to hear Him clearly. He longs to talk to you!

Seek Outwardly
If you have time, read 1 Samuel 3:1-10. Then, write in your journal the words from verse 10: "Speak, for your servant is listening." Wait for Him to speak to you. As you begin to hear your Husband's voice, write in your journal what He says to you. The more you walk with Him, the more you will be able to distinguish His voice. Be patient and stay attentive to hear Him.

Day 4: Parental Guidance

Try to get outdoors in God's creation again today. Ask Him to reveal His presence to you and to teach you more about Him as you spend this time with Him.

. . . .

Growing up, I got my share of spankings. I totally deserved every one of them! My mother made sure that it hurt me enough to remember it the next time I thought about being disobedient. Oh, how I may have turned out if it weren't for a mother who loved me enough to punish me when I needed it!

As your Husband seeks to partner with you to perfect you, He will offer you His precepts, principles, promises, and His Spirit to help you. But you can choose to ignore His commands, disregard His heart, and reject His Spirit, walking in your own selfishness and pride.

Read Isaiah 53:6 and record in your journal who we are like and why.

> We all, like sheep, have gone astray,
>   each of us has turned to our own way. — Isaiah 53:6

When we choose to turn away from God, it leaves our Father no other choice but to respond in His justice and holiness by imposing discipline upon us for our disobedience.

Read Hebrews 12:5-6,9-11 in your Bible and write in your journal what this verse says to you.

> My child, don't make light of the Lord's discipline,
>   and don't give up when he corrects you.
> For the Lord disciplines those he loves,
>   and he punishes each one he accepts as his child. . . .

Since we respected our earthly fathers who disciplined us, shouldn't we submit even more to the discipline of the Father of our spirits, and live forever?

For our earthly fathers disciplined us for a few years, doing the best they knew how. But God's discipline is always good for us, so that we might share in his holiness. No discipline is enjoyable while it is happening—it's painful! But afterward there will be a peaceful harvest of right living for those who are trained in this way.
—Hebrews 12:5-6,9-11, NLT

In Hebrews 12:6, the word *punish* means "to impose a penalty" while the word *discipline* means "the act of punishing." A lot of people don't like the word *punish*. They think it is too harsh and makes God sound mean. They believe that God doesn't punish us, but instead just lets us suffer the consequences of our bad choices.

As a parent, I have spanked my children only to hear them say, "You're mean, Mommy!" Many times, my response was, "Am I mean or are you disobedient?" So often, we make God out to be the bad guy, when in reality we made the choice and He just responded. What would happen if a child was allowed to hit her parents continually and was never disciplined for it? Would that lack of discipline be fair to the child? Would excusing the child's behavior help that child become mature? Absolutely not! If not disciplined, that child would grow up to believe that her behavior was okay and that God was okay with it. How distorted is that?

In God's holiness and justice, He imposes a penalty for our disobedient, independent living apart from Him, as sheep who are prone to wander off. Many times, the discipline may very well be suffering the natural consequences that result from our choices, but nonetheless, it is discipline and punishment. If God didn't punish, then He would not be just or holy, which then makes Him no longer good, because He is not showing fairness, making Him no longer loving.

Even in the midst of discipline and punishment, God is also merciful and gracious. In Jeremiah 21:14, God said, "I will punish you as your deeds deserve," but Psalm 103:10 says, "He does not treat us as our sins deserve or repay us according to our iniquities." They sound a little contradictory, don't they? Not if you understand the character of your all-encompassing, never-changing Husband! He is loving, good, just, holy, merciful, and gracious all at the same time. In Jeremiah, God was declaring His punishment that would be imposed should His people choose to be disobedient. In Psalms, He wasn't offering not to punish *at all*, but rather was not giving the full extent of the justice they really deserved. That is God's mercy. In God's holiness and justice, He will impose a punishment, but His goodness, mercy, and grace toward the one He loves compels Him to temper His justice.

Wrapping It Up

Be grateful for the Lord's discipline. He loves you enough to correct your wrongdoing and to partner in your spiritual growth. How gracious He is to not give you the full measure of what your disobedience deserves, because of His deep mercy. In His omniscience, He knows exactly what kind of discipline you need to set you on the right course for your future. That's what He applies to you—just what it will take to turn your heart back to Him.

Loving Response

Seek Upwardly

What would happen if we had no laws in our society? What if we had no traffic lights? There would be wrecks everywhere! What if people didn't have to pay a fine for speeding? Would they slow down? I think not! The most loving thing your Husband can do in His perfecting process with you is to set before you His commands, give you the Holy Spirit to help you, and discipline you to learn from your mistakes. As you drive through your town today and see stop signs or traffic signals, thank your Groom for His commands, His Spirit, and His discipline.

Seek Inwardly

In your journal, write the words from Proverbs 3:12: "The LORD disciplines those he loves." Discipline is truly one of the most loving things He could do. Take some time to pour out your heart to God. Maybe today you could even thank Him for His loving rebuke and discipline.

Seek Outwardly

Look back at the verses from Hebrews 12. Draw some flowers or some fruit in your journal to show that God promises a harvest of right living and peace when discipline is viewed as God's loving act for growing us into His likeness.

Day 5: Spirit Power

Find another quiet place for you and God out in His creation. Ask Him to guide you and speak to you as you complete this week of study.

. . . .

This week, you have learned that Jesus Christ, your Husband, longs to partner with you, offering His precepts, principles, promises, and His Spirit, the Paraclete. Should you choose to disobey, He chastises you because He loves you deeply and wants to see you truly happy. You may see the walk of obedience to His commands as a daunting task that feels impossible. The good news is that not only did God give you the Holy Spirit to help you, but He gave you the Holy Spirit to empower you! God never expects you to try to walk in obedience by yourself. He placed His Spirit inside of you to give you the power to overcome your sinful desires and live by the Spirit.

How many people do you know who are Christians but try to live the Christian life on their own, apart from Christ? I know a bunch! They strive with all their might to live like Jesus, and yet they fall short; they are exhausted, frustrated, and disillusioned with Christianity, because they have not surrendered themselves to the partnership and power that the Holy Spirit offers.

In Zechariah 4:6, the Lord said, "Not by might nor by power, but by my Spirit." You can try to live the Christian life on your own, but you will be miserable. God never intended for You to walk alone. Your Husband wants to partner with you, walking hand in hand as a couple, as He perfects you.

Open your Bible and read Galatians 3:3. Note why Paul rebuked the Galatians.

> Are you so foolish? After beginning by means of the Spirit, are you now trying to finish by means of the flesh? —Galatians 3:3

How did you come to understand your need for Christ? According to John 6:44, the Father drew you. How did you come to Christ? By faith. A moment came in which you believed in Christ and accepted His death as payment for your sin, and relied on His resurrection, His presence, and His Spirit to give you life (see Romans 3:22). Once you join Christ, how are you perfected, becoming more like Christ? By the power of the Holy Spirit (see Romans 15:16). How do you keep from living in your flesh? By living and walking in the Spirit (see Galatians 5:16). How do you bear fruit? By the power of the Spirit (see Galatians 5:22-25). Where does your hope come from? The Holy Spirit (see Romans 15:13). I could go on and on, but I think you get the point. The power to become all that God desires for you to be comes from the Spirit.

And how strong is this power? "That you may know . . . his incomparably great power for us who believe. That power is the same as the mighty strength he exerted when he raised Christ from the dead" (Ephesians 1:18-20). The power given to you by the Holy Spirit's dwelling in you is the same power that raised Jesus from the dead. Is there anything the Spirit can't do? Absolutely not!

Wrapping It Up

As your Partner is perfecting you, His Spirit comes alongside you and reminds you of His precepts, principles, and promises. But He will hand you over to yourself (see Romans 1:24) if you absolutely and intentionally choose to willingly disobey Him. He does discipline and punish you, but He takes no pleasure in doing it. His holiness makes Him just. If He doesn't let you suffer the consequences of your wrong behavior, then you would continue in that sinful behavior, so it is actually His love and goodness that motivates His chastisement. His mercy doesn't let it go further than it needs to in order to get your attention, and His grace offers forgiveness when you confess and repent. This is the character of your "better half" Husband who says to you, "I am going to give you the principles, but I am also going to give you a *Paraclete* to help you and the power to live them out. I am with you. And My presence offers you all you need."

Loving Response
Seek Upwardly

In your journal, write the words from John 16:7: "But very truly I tell you, it is for your good that I am going away. Unless I go away, the Advocate will not come to you; but if I go, I will send him to you." Journal your heart to your Groom, thanking Him for sending you a Partner in the Holy Spirit. Confess the times you have not partnered with Him, and surrender your life afresh to partner with your *Paraclete*.

Seek Inwardly

Talk with God about your attempts to live like Christ in your own power and not by the Spirit's power. Ask Him to give you the strength you need to call upon the Spirit's help and live by the Spirit's power instead of your own.

Seek Outwardly

Trace your hand in your journal. On each finger, write these words: Precepts (on your thumb), Principles (on your index finger), Promises (on your middle finger), Paraclete (on your ring finger), and Power (on your pinky). Now use your own hand to recite these words, folding your fingers down as you say them. If you will notice, you just formed a fist.

With these five partnering elements active in your life, you can punch out the flesh that works independently from God, destroying sin and self, becoming perfected as you walk with your Husband.

As you think about what you learned about God this week, try to capture that in a picture, song lyrics, or art. Bring it, along with your journal, to your next meeting so you can share all that God is doing in your heart and life.

a journey less traveled

Day 1: God Is Not a Critic

Spend time with God out in nature again today. Ask His Spirit to help you understand more of who He really is.

· · · · · · · · ·

"I am my own worst critic." So often, I have heard this phrase, communicating that most of the time you think your performance is worse than others would think. But many have lived with far worse criticism than they would have ever given themselves, leaving them feeling useless and worthless.

If you experienced a judgmental and critical upbringing, you may have allowed that experience to trickle down into your perception of God. If you had an earthly father who was constantly criticizing your every action, who felt cold and distant, and who was unwilling or unable to empathize with you or anyone else, you may take on this mental image of God.

If you view God as critical, how might it make you feel? Perhaps you would feel like you will never measure up, so you give up trying to pursue Him. Maybe you feel as if He is sitting up in the far reaches of heaven on His throne just waiting to throw down His wrath on you. You might think He is cold, distant, emotionless, and rigid. Who wants to draw near to that kind of deity?

Choosing to define God like this can be devastating to your future with Him and your response to others. This misperception of God may send you to one of two extremes: You will work really, really hard just to avoid His weighty critique of you, or you will just quit altogether in total hopelessness. God doesn't want either of those things to happen.

Unfortunately, many people see God as cold, distant, harsh, and critical. They think He has no emotion other than anger. This misconception results in an unhealthy fear of Him—as if He were waiting for just the right time to take you out.

People who are cold, distant, judgmental, and hard have never learned to empathize with others. To show empathy is to put yourself in another's shoes and consider how she feels. People who show empathy are full of compassion and consideration. They will think about another's feelings and not just their own. People who do not think about the feelings of others usually will find themselves very alone because others can't connect or draw close to them.

The truth is that people who are critical and lack empathy are usually unhappy with themselves. They see so many things in themselves that they don't like and therefore criticize others in an attempt to make themselves feel better.

This is not God's character. God is not cold, distant, judgmental, and hard. God is a perfect example of empathy.

Read Psalm 103:14 and write in your journal what you find.

> For he knows how we are formed,
>   he remembers that we are dust. — Psalm 103:14

The psalmist declares that God knows you very well and personally feels your pain.

Read Psalm 56:8 (one of my favorites!) and record what it tells you about the character of your God.

> You keep track of all my sorrows.
> You have collected all my tears in your bottle.
> You have recorded each one in your book.
> —Psalm 56:8, NLT

I hope it brings you much comfort to know that God both holds and records all your tears as you struggle in life.

Wrapping It Up

God is a deeply emotional God who empathized with you enough to die for you. His death and resurrection offers you the life He desires for you because He knows you, understands you, and feels your pain. Your Husband is so full of compassion for you that He stopped at nothing to win your love, all because He wants to connect with you deeply, in a way that you have never experienced in limited human relationships.

Loving Response

Seek Upwardly

As you have been learning today more of who God really is, write these words across your journal: "God Is Not a Critic." Then, take a moment to write your thoughts about what you have just learned. Maybe you need to confess that you have felt this way toward God. Maybe you need to repent of this misconception of Him and invite Him to show you who He really is.

Seek Inwardly

Write Psalm 56:8 in your journal. Talk to your Husband about how thankful you are that He cares for you and empathizes for you the way He does. Ask Him if you lack empathy with Him, and what empathizing with Him even looks like.

Seek Outwardly

Create a heart from a piece of construction paper (or open the envelope given to you). Write "I Understand" on that heart and carry it around with you today as a reminder. Try to memorize Psalm 56:8. You may find that you need the reminder, or someone whose path you cross may desperately need to know this truth. Think about if you need to learn to empathize with others the way God has empathized with you. Ask God to help you model His empathy toward those around you.

At the end of the day, put the heart in your box and let it serve as a reminder of who God really is.

Day 2: God Is Passionate

Sit out in nature today and look for God to reveal Himself to you. Invite His Spirit to teach you what He wants you to learn.

. . . .

In today's society, the first leap our thoughts may make is that the word *passionate* insinuates some kind of sexual act. Far from it! The word *passion* simply means a "strong feeling or emotion." The term can even be applied to God's character. God does not lack feeling or passion. God is extremely passionate, and He has been since the day He created you. His passionate love created you, wooed you, saved you, and remains with you.

Where does passion originate? God is passionate about what He created. But, how do we become passionate about anything? Many of us develop passion from our pain. Strong emotion that often results in crusades and callings sometimes stems from our own pain, because we want to save others from what we went through. There can be no passion without compassion. Compassion means to understand the suffering of another and to want to do something about it. Compassion causes you to identify with another. When you do, you develop a passion so strong that action must take place.

I think about my children. When they are happy, I'm happy. When they are sad, I'm sad. When someone hurts them, I am ready to take up an offense and come to their rescue. Why? Because I have a deep relationship with them and a deep compassion for them. I can identify with them. Out of that, I develop strong emotions that move me into action.

One of the first Scriptures about the compassion and passion of Jesus is recorded in Matthew 9:36. If you have your Bible, find this verse and underline it.

> When he saw the crowds, he had compassion on them, because
> they were harassed and helpless, like sheep without a shepherd.
> —Matthew 9:36

Jesus saw the people He loved—those who were to be His bride—suffering loneliness and exhaustion, with no one to lovingly lead them. He identified with their feelings, igniting a deep passion to help. Immediately, He told the disciples to pray for more leaders who would come help. Then, in Matthew 10, He drew the disciples together and gave them the power to go help them.

Wrapping It Up

God's passion toward you comes from His deep compassion for you. God made you and thus knows you intimately, even better than you know yourself. He understands all that you face and all that you go through, and He has strong emotions for and toward you.

Loving Response

Seek Upwardly

In your journal, record these words from Psalm 145:8: "The LORD is gracious, and full of compassion" (KJV). Look at the box you started using at the beginning of our time together. That thing ought to be pretty full by now. When something is full, it contains as much as it possibly can. Ponder the fact as it applies to God. Your Husband contains all the consideration, empathy, and compassion for you that He can possibly hold. He feels what you feel so deeply that He is moved to action.

Seek Inwardly

Here's something else for you to think about: If your Husband has feelings, isn't it possible that you have neglected them? So often, we forget that God's heart is moved by our actions, good or bad. But God does feel deeply. Have you ever considered His feelings? Have you ever considered how your actions might make your Husband feel? Talk with Him about this and journal your heart to Him. This week, as you fill a glass, a bowl, your purse, or your gas tank, remember that your Husband is full of compassion. He understands how you feel and desires to passionately do something about it.

Seek Outwardly
Write "God Is Passionate" on a piece of paper and stick it in your box to remind you of this truth during the week.

Day 3: To the Rescue!

The Bible says that the earth is full of God's glory (see Isaiah 6:3). Since the earth contains all of God's glory that it possibly can, try to spend time in His creation and let Him reveal His glory to you.

· · · · · · · · ·

In the 1950s, an animated cartoon known as *Mighty Mouse* came to television with a catchy little theme song that said, "Here he comes to save the day!" It was Mighty Mouse to the rescue! And he stayed around rescuing for thirty years. We like the story of rescue a lot. One of the greatest parts of any love story is when the beauty is rescued. Think of the movies where rescue is the prevailing theme. There is something entirely romantic about rescue.

Your Husband is so compassionate toward you that He passionately rescues His bride. Throughout Scripture, the Bible speaks of rescue but uses it very differently than the limited definition we place on that word. The word *rescue* is the translation for several different words in both Hebrew (what the Old Testament was originally written in) and Greek (what the New Testament was originally written in). In the Old Testament, one Hebrew word for "rescue" is *shuwb* and has a broad meaning, including "return, come back to, turn back to, bring back to, and restore." This definition is applied when we have walked away from God and He is asking us to return; it is also used when we have lost the consciousness of and thus our confidence in God's presence, and we are asking Him to return to us.

Open your Bible and read Psalm 35:17 to see an example of the word being used.

> How long, O Lord, will you look on and do nothing?
> Rescue me from their fierce attacks.
> Protect my life from these lions! —Psalm 35:17, NLT

David was asking for an awareness of God's presence to return to him because he felt alone and vulnerable. He was saying, "Lord, please return to me and restore me and You, because I need You in order to overcome my enemy."

Now Read Zechariah 1:3 and see how the same word is used.

> Therefore, say to the people, "This is what the LORD of Heaven's Armies says: Return to me, and I will return to you, says the LORD of Heaven's Armies."—Zechariah 1:3, NLT

In this verse, the prophet Zechariah proclaimed that God was asking His people to return to relationship with Him. Then He would do the same. Your Husband is a gentleman. He will not make Himself known where He is not welcomed, wanted, or invited.

In the New Testament, a Greek word for "rescue" is *rhyomai* and means "to draw to one's self, to rescue, to deliver." This is applied when we have unwarranted and unprovoked enemies who are coming against us. Notice that the definition doesn't contain the word "yank" or "quickly." Sometimes rescue takes time.

In 2 Thessalonians 3:2, Paul said, "Pray, too, that we will be rescued from wicked and evil people, for not everyone is a believer" (NLT). Paul asked God to draw him close, to rescue him, and to deliver him from ungodly people who tried to hurt him. We can pray the same for our own lives.

In 2 Timothy 4:18 Paul wrote, "The Lord will rescue me from every evil attack and will bring me safely to his heavenly kingdom. To him be glory for ever and ever. Amen." Paul was implying that the Lord will draw us to Himself and deliver us from evil attacks.

Think about your current circumstances. You may be experiencing a situation in which God could rescue you, and yet feel as though He is choosing not to. Many times, that feeling of abandonment comes because we think rescue always means *relief.* If that is our only definition for *rescue*, then we will be severely disappointed in God when He doesn't provide us instant relief the minute life gets tough.

God's primary concern for you is not your relief. Your Husband is after a relationship with you. As a matter of fact, He will not provide relief until you humble yourself and return to Him. Sometimes He rescues us from ourselves. This is the deeper definition of rescue.

Look at those in the Bible who needed rescue. David was in desperate need of rescue when King Saul was trying to kill him. In the Psalms, he begged for God to rescue him. God sent David's friend Jonathan for support, and 1 Samuel 23:16 says that Jonathan "strengthened his hand in God" (RSV). God did not give David relief from Saul; he kept running for his life and hiding in caves. Eventually, God did offer him rescue by sending a dear friend to give him the strength he needed to make it through. God may not always give you relief, but He may use those around you to strengthen your hand in God. In these times God is still rescuing you. It just might not be the kind of rescue you were expecting.

Later, David sinned against God as he lusted after Bathsheba, committed adultery with her, and then had her husband killed in order to cover it up and take her for himself. In Psalm 51:12, David cried out to God, "Restore to me the joy of your salvation." The word "restore" is *shuwb*. David no longer felt God's presence and was saying, "Return to me; come back to me, God; I need a consciousness of Your presence."

Wrapping It Up

Make no mistake about it. Your Husband feels so deeply toward you that His compassion stirs within Him a passion to rescue you. And just because it isn't always instant relief doesn't mean it isn't rescue.

Loving Response

Seek Upwardly

Take some time to meditate on the fact that your Husband passionately rescues you. Ask Him to show you ways that He has rescued you in the past. Ask Him to show you how He is rescuing you even now and you've missed it. Thank Him for being so compassionate that He would passionately come to your rescue by causing you to return to Him, turn back to Him, and be restored to right relationship with Him in His loving presence. Thank your Husband for rescuing you from yourself.

Seek Inwardly

Your Husband also rescues you from the enemy and others who declare war against you. In your journal, personalize and record this verse in your own words: "Whenever we are faced with any calamity such as war, plague, or famine, we can come to stand in your presence.... We can cry out to you to save us, and you will hear us and rescue us" (2 Chronicles 20:9, NLT).

Thank God that whatever you are facing now or in your future, He will rescue you from the hand of your enemy. Cry out to Him and ask Him to rescue you from the circumstances you are currently facing. Declare that your Husband has promised to restore you, deliver you, strengthen you, and free you from the enemies you face. Walk in that confidence.

Seek Outwardly

Psalm 20:7 says, "Some nations boast of their chariots and horses, but we boast in the name of the LORD our God" (NLT). Sometime today, make it a point to boast in your Husband who passionately rescues you by telling someone how He has rescued you in your life.

Day 4: Covering for a Rainy Day

Try to sit outside again today or get near a window and take in creation. Thank Him for the love He gives you as He is present with you and is passionately pursuing you.

. . . .

It was the fall of 2009. High school football game. Not a sign of rain. Without notice, the bottom drops out and everyone races to their cars. I am carrying our seats, attempting to use them as a makeshift umbrella. When I finally arrive at the car, my family locks the car doors and proceeds to yell, "Dance, Mama, Dance!" No arguing, begging, or bargaining is working, so in front of several hundred people, I have to "shake my wet booty" in order to get out of the rain. I get in the car and ride home, soaked to the bone and looking like a wet rat, because I was unprepared and unprotected from the storm.

Your Husband is so compassionate that He not only passionately rescues His bride, but He also passionately protects His bride. Psalm 5:11 says,

> But let all who take refuge in you be glad;
>> let them ever sing for joy.
> Spread your protection over them,
>> that those who love your name may rejoice in you.

The word *protection* is *cakak* and means "to hedge, fence about; to block, overshadow, screen; to cover; to lay over."

In the New Testament, the word for *protection* is *stego*, meaning "to thatch, to cover, to protect or keep by covering, to preserve; to keep secret, to hide, conceal the errors and faults of others." This is exactly what happened when Jesus died for us and the Bible says that His blood "covers" our sin. His blood thatched the hole that sin brought in our lives. His blood preserved our life. His blood conceals all of our errors and faults, just like a permanent black marker completely and permanently covers.

How do you think God protects us? According to the Bible, God protects us with His presence and thus His love.

Read 1 Corinthians 13:7 and list what love does in your journal.

> [Love] always protects, always trusts, always hopes, always perseveres.
> —1 Corinthians 13:7

God's love always (that ought to give you some confidence!) protects because where you find love, you find God's presence. His presence allows Him to see us and have compassion for us, responding in passion to protect us. See how all of who God is comes together?

Look up Proverbs 18:10 in your Bible and see where we can find confidence in His protection.

> The name of the Lord is a fortified tower;
>   the righteous run to it and are safe.
> —Proverbs 18:10

Throughout this study, we have discovered who God really is as well as some of His specific names spelled out in Scripture. God's name gives us the confidence that His loving presence is with us to protect us. He is known as the Wonderful Counselor, Prince of Peace, Redeemer, Healer, Provider, and so much more. We can know that His names give us a fortified covering of protection that we can run and stand up under.

What do we gain by His passionate protection? We gain refuge and rest. Psalm 46:1 says, "God is our refuge and strength, an ever-present help in trouble." The word *refuge* is *machaceh* and means "a shelter from rain or storm, from danger, and from falsehood."

Psalm 91:1 says, "Those who live in the shelter of the Most High will find rest in the shadow of the Almighty" (NLT). The word *rest* in this verse can also be translated as "abide" and is the Hebrew word *luwn*. This word means "to lodge, to remain, and to make to rest."

Wrapping It Up

When the rainstorms of life come, God takes action to protect you because of His compassion for you. When you remain under God's covering, you can rest in the assurance that His loving presence protects you.

Loving Response

Seek Upwardly

Have you ever picked up a bird's feather off the ground? Psalm 91:4 says, "He will cover you with his feathers, and under his wings you will find refuge." Trace or draw a feather in your journal and write the Scripture out to the side. Journal your heart to God, thanking Him for being so compassionate that He would passionately protect you from sin and evil, much like a mother bird protects her babies.

Seek Inwardly

Talk with God about times when you felt that He didn't protect you. Let Him speak to you about those times. You may need to release those times in surrender to your Husband, declaring your trust in Him. What name of God do you need to be a strong tower for you?

Seek Outwardly

If you have a feather, you may want to carry it around with you today as a visible reminder that your Husband protects you. As you go, share with others about God's protection. You may even offer to them a name of God that they need for the circumstances they face. At the end of the day, place your feather in your box as another reminder of who God is.

For home economics in high school, we had to care for an egg for an entire week. It was hard to keep that egg from cracking! Just as we carefully protected that fragile egg, God will protect your fragile heart. Sometimes we experience heartbreak that feels like we can't go on, but God knows us better than we know ourselves. Our Groom is our protector. He can be trusted.

Day 5: Extending

Find another quiet place for you and God out in His creation. Ask Him to guide you and speak to you as this week of study draws to a close.

• • • • • • • • •

Several years ago our family went with a group of families to a resort in Tennessee. They had a three-story ropes course available to build teamwork. The goal was to get yourself across each of the obstacles, moving higher as you go. You were not allowed to hold on to anything, only other people's hands as they were extended to you. I learned real quickly how special an extended hand was to my soul!

Read 2 Chronicles 5:7-9 and write down what you find that was extended.

> Then the priests carried the Ark of the LORD's Covenant into the inner sanctuary of the Temple — the Most Holy Place — and placed it beneath the wings of the cherubim. The cherubim spread their wings over the Ark, forming a canopy over the Ark and its carrying poles. These poles were so long that their ends could be seen from the Temple's main room — the Holy Place — but not from the outside. They are still there to this day. — 2 Chronicles 5:7-9, NLT

The Holy Spirit revealed to me that when I accepted Jesus Christ, He became my Husband. Our covenant relationship, based on Him being a Promise-Keeper, brought me into a sacred relationship with Him. His deep love for me allowed me to be in His presence and under His protection, just like the Ark of the Covenant remained under the protection of the cherubim. Just as the poles of the Ark of the Covenant extended out beyond the Holy of Holies for others to see as evidence of God's presence, God desires for me to extend His life and love to others so they can see evidence of what it is like to have a deep, loving relationship with Him. Many of us miss that aspect of knowing God. We *receive* all of who God is for us, but we never *extend* it to others. Those who dare to do this embark on an exciting adventure with their Husband. And it is often a journey less traveled by most.

If I am going to take this journey less traveled, I must ask myself a few questions: Do I have empathy for others? Do I have compassion for others? Out of that compassion, do I have a passion to extend the love of Jesus to others?

Read Colossians 3:12 and record what Paul says we are to do.

> Therefore, as God's chosen people, holy and dearly loved, clothe yourselves with compassion, kindness, humility, gentleness and patience. — Colossians 3:12

Now read Philippians 2:1-4 and record what you find there.

> Therefore if you have any encouragement from being united with Christ, if any comfort from his love, if any common sharing in the Spirit, if any tenderness and compassion, then make my joy complete by being like-minded, having the same love, being one in spirit and of one mind. Do nothing out of selfish ambition or vain conceit. Rather, in humility value others above yourselves, not looking to your own interests but each of you to the interests of the others. — Philippians 2:1-4

Because your Husband feels so deeply toward you and others, He wants you to both understand and experience His passion for you and then offer that same passion and compassion to others who need it. He wants you clothed with the same love that you have received from Him.

Go to blueletterbible.com and dissect 1 Peter 1:22, using the feature that will allow you to look at the original words and their meanings.

> Now that you have purified yourselves by obeying the truth so that you have sincere love for each other, love one another deeply, from the heart. — 1 Peter 1:22

Then, in your journal, paraphrase the verse in your own words based on what each word means. Note: "The truth" used in that verse is Jesus' command to love one another as He has loved you (see John 13:34).

Here's what I wrote: "Because I am no longer loving others with the fleshly, carnal, worldly love that is empty and self-seeking, and I am obeying Your command to 'love one another' so that I have brotherly love that is pure and not fake, I now need to love them with God-like, sacrificial love, striving to do this with all that is in me."

Wrapping It Up

Your Husband loves you deeply, sincerely, and passionately. You are in the forefront of His mind all of the time, extending to you compassion, kindness, gentleness, and patience. He now calls you to extend that kind of love — His love — to others.

Loving Response

Seek Upwardly

Talk with your Husband about what you have learned this week. Thank Him for being so passionate about you. Thank Him for being your Rescuer and Protecter. Choose one of the Scriptures in today's study that speaks the most to you. Write it in your journal and try to memorize it, so you'll have it when you need it.

Seek Inwardly

Because your Husband is passionate about people, He wants us to be that way as well. Talk with God about who you can show His passionate love to and how you can share it with others.

Seek Outwardly

Ask Him to reveal to you what abilities He has given you that may be used to love and help others. Then, jump in with both feet, trusting that He will provide all you need and will guide you all the way.

In your box, you have now placed who God is to you as your Husband: Present, Pursuer, Promise-Keeper, Perfecter, Partner, and Passionate. Take some time to pull each of those names out of the box and consider how God might want to use you to portray those character traits to others.

Think about what you learned about who God is this week. Seek to capture that in a picture, song lyrics, or art. Bring it along with your journal to your next group meeting so you can share all that God is doing in your heart and life.

week 7

and they lived happily ever after

Day 1: God Is Not a Hypocrite

Find the song "Gloria" by Watermark. Then, go outside and listen to the song. Soak in all that nature is doing in an effort to praise your Husband today. Let it convict you to do the same with your life, and let it challenge you to praise Him fully throughout your day.

• • • • • • • • •

One of the most prevalent and insidious characteristics that gets projected onto God is hypocrisy. The origin of the word *hypocrite* actually comes from the ancient Greek theater and refers to actors who pretend to be someone that they were not. Today, this word still carries that same definition: pretending to be someone you are not. Fake.

Hypocrisy is a huge indictment against the church. Many say that churchgoers are the most hypocritical of all. The problem with this statement is that it lumps and dumps everybody into that category when that is not the case for many. The argument is that the people who go to church do not conduct themselves like Jesus would. Here is my response: That's why we go to church! Most people visit a church because something is missing in their lives and they need to find out if Jesus will fill the void. Most people faithfully attend church because they desire to know Jesus and how He lived so they can live like Him. They also want and need the fellowship of other Christians to encourage them in the journey of walking with Him and becoming more like Him. Going to church does not make you perfect any more than going to McDonald's makes you a hamburger! We go to church to worship God for all He has done for us, and to learn *how* to be more like Jesus as we learn to walk with Him, not to pretend to *be* Jesus. It is not a game, it is a relationship.

Read and meditate on Philippians 3:13-14.

> No, dear brothers and sisters, I have not achieved it, but I focus on this one thing: Forgetting the past and looking forward to what lies ahead, I press on to reach the end of the race and receive the heavenly prize for which God, through Christ Jesus, is calling us.
> — Philippians 3:13-14, NLT

Now, granted, some people certainly go to church regularly and yet continue to live less than they have been taught to live. Sure, some people attend church and pretend to be perfect on Sundays but act differently during the rest of the week. Some try to be like Christ by their own self-effort, while others don't try at all. But to lump and dump that on the church as a whole is unfair. For the sincere Christian, there is nothing pretend or fake about their desire to be like Jesus, and they feel sincere remorse when they "mess up."

Paul took his relationship with God extremely seriously, striving to be just like Christ, but still said about himself: "I am the chief of sinners" (1 Timothy 1:15).

True, sincere Christians don't pretend to be like Christ; they pursue Christlikeness. And when they miss the mark, God offers them the gift of forgiveness and second (and third, and fourth, and . . .) chances.

Wrapping It Up

God is not a hypocrite. God does not say one thing in His Word and then act differently. He is not a fake or a pretend God. He is who He says He is and He does what He says He will do. God is present, pursuing, promise-keeping, perfecting, partnering, and passionate consistently and eternally. It is part of His DNA, so to speak. He can't cease to be any of these things always and forever. God is the same yesterday, today, and forever (see Hebrews 13:8).

God is not a hypocrite. God is and always will be exactly who He says He is.

Loving Response

Seek Upwardly

Take a moment to talk with God about how you might have accused Him of being a hypocrite. Confess to the Lord if you have viewed all people in the church as hypocrites, or if you have allowed a few who have acted hypocritically to jade your view of the church. Journal your heart to your Groom.

Seek Inwardly

Talk with God by asking yourself these questions: Am I hypocritical? In what areas? How can I change my thoughts about that so my behavior will better reflect the truth about Jesus?

Seek Outwardly

In your journal, write "God Is Not a Hypocrite." You may want to draw a theatrical mask and put a big *X* over it. Beside this, write these words from Hebrews 13:8: "Jesus Christ is the same yesterday and today and forever." Think on that verse throughout the day and allow your Husband to affirm in you the steady confidence and security that He is for you. He never changes. You don't have to wonder if He will love or leave, commit or cheat. He is and always will be your Husband, if you will just let Him. Share with others that God can be their security too.

Day 2: God Is Permanent and Faithful

Try to get outside to sit in nature and look for God to reveal Himself to you. Invite His Spirit to guide you into His truth.

. . . .

Many years ago, we had our house repainted. Our son, at the age of twelve, thought it neat to touch the white, wet paint and then leave his handprint on the red brick. Though much scrubbing has taken place, there is a permanent handprint on our home that will last as long as the house does!

Your Husband is permanent. He is not going anywhere. He is continuing and enduring, totally incapable of changing any aspect of His character. God's permanence is so difficult for us to fathom because we, as imperfect people, are always changing. Yet, He is perfect. His love is perfect. Both His character and His commitment never change. He can be counted on to remain the same yesterday, today, and forever.

Throughout the Old Testament, Scripture after Scripture speaks about the faithfulness of God. From the parting of the Red Sea to the manna from heaven, God's miracles proved to His people that He could be counted on because He was faithful. He was proving His faithfulness because they would need to rely on that faithfulness to make it to and then live in the Promised Land. His faithfulness convinced the people and made them confident. Nearly every Scripture coupled God's faithfulness with His unfailing love.

Open your Bible and read Psalm 89:2. Note what it says about God's love and faithfulness.

> Your unfailing love will last forever.
> Your faithfulness is as enduring as the heavens.
> —Psalm 89:2, NLT

God's faithfulness and love are always coupled together. Whenever you experience God's unfailing love, He is present because God is love. And God's presence demonstrates His faithfulness to you. Conversely, His faithfulness provides proof of His unfailing love and His presence. Love and faithfulness go hand in hand. In God, you can't have one without the other. (If we, as people, could grasp this, there would be much better marriages than we see today!)

In the New Testament, Jesus offered miracle after miracle to prove His faithfulness to His disciples. He would often say something like, "Oh, you of little faith!" He wanted His disciples to know that He could be trusted. Jesus also demonstrated His faithfulness to His bride (His followers).

Read John 10:3-5,10 and list all the ways that you see God's faithfulness to you.

> [The Good Shepherd] calls his own sheep by name and leads them out. When he has brought out all his own, he goes on ahead of them, and his sheep follow him because they know his voice. But they will never follow a stranger; in fact, they will run away from him because they do not recognize a stranger's voice. . . . I have come that they may have life, and have it to the full. — John 10:3-5,10

Jesus proved Himself to be a good Shepherd whose sheep hear His voice, recognize His voice, and follow Him. As Jesus proved Himself trustworthy to the sheep, they refused to follow a stranger. Jesus was no stranger to the sheep. They knew Him and He knew them, and they were convinced and confident that He could be trusted. To this day, Jesus has been proving Himself faithful so we can live the abundant life that He planned for us as we live in His presence and thus in His love. Again, His unfailing love and faithfulness go hand in hand.

While on earth, Jesus was constantly proving His unfailing love and His faithfulness to us. The ultimate demonstration of His faithful love was His death on the cross for us. His resurrection proved He conquered death and defeated our sin. This allows us to experience the abundant life that comes with walking in His presence and love, moment by moment. He knows we will face obstacles as we head toward the promised land of eternity, so He prepares us — just like He did our spiritual forefathers — by showing us His unfailing love and faithfulness. This convinces us and thus gives us the confidence we need to face whatever comes our way. He is with us, He loves us, and He is for us!

Wrapping It Up

As today's study concludes, here's something beautiful for you to see about your Husband. Revelation 19:11 says, "Then I saw heaven opened, and a white horse was standing there. Its rider was named Faithful and True" (NLT). From the beginning of creation to the end of time (Revelation), God has proven Himself faithful.

Loving Response

Seek Upwardly

Take some time and talk with God about His permanence. Thank Him for His faithfulness. Thank Him that His faithfulness convinces you of His unfailing love and constant presence, and gives you confidence to live each day, knowing that He is faithful to His character and His commitment to you.

Seek Inwardly

Write these words from Psalm 146:6 in your journal: "He remains faithful forever" (HCSB). Then journal your heart to your Groom. Talk with Him about your faithfulness to Him, in return. Are you faithful? Why or why not? How can you be more faithful to God?

Seek Outwardly

You may want to take a permanent marker and write *faithful,* or πιστός (as it looks in Greek) somewhere that will serve as a continual reminder that He is permanent and faithful. Take the time to share with others how permanent and faithful God is. So many need to hear that truth.

Write the phrase "God Is Permanent" on a piece of paper and stick it in your box to remind you of this truth during the week.

Day 3: Do You Trust Him?

As you sit out in nature today, ask your Father to declare to you who He is through what He created. Ask the Holy Spirit to speak, lead, teach, and come alongside you as you spend this time with Him.

· · · · · · · · ·

God has proven over and over again that He is faithful. But what about you? Are you faithful? Do you have faith in Him?

In today's culture, nothing is believed unless it can be thoroughly explained. A wave of intellectualism is moving through our society, demanding concrete evidence as a prerequisite of belief. God did create our brains, and He created them to be used, but not to create barriers to faith. Often, when we can't explain God and His ways, our faith begins to waver. In those times, we trust our limited intellect instead of trusting in our God who is so magnificent that our minds cannot comprehend Him!

When we get to a place where we need explanations for everything, we have just nullified faith. One of the words for "faith" in the Bible is *pistis*, which means to "believe God to the point of conviction and action; complete trust." James MacDonald says that faith is "believing the Word of God and acting on it no matter how you feel because He always promises a good result." Faith chooses to believe despite the absence of evidence.

Read Hebrews 11:1, and write this definition of faith in your journal.

> Now faith is confidence in what we hope for and assurance about what we do not see. — Hebrews 11:1

Think about this for a minute: If something can be seen, then it ceases to require faith. So, for the most part, we spend most of our time trying to get ourselves to a place where we don't need faith. Yet

God tells us that without faith, it is impossible to please God (see Hebrews 11:6).

The rest of Hebrews 11 tells the stories of people who lived by faith. Even Jesus lived by faith, as He trusted His Daddy so much that He died for His bride. He trusted that His death would bring salvation and unite us to Him.

So, the question remains: Do you have faith in Him?

Are you trusting that your ever-present, always-loving Husband is faithful, and therefore He can be completely trusted in unlimited abandonment of your heart to Him? This trusting led to your salvation. You declared that you were trusting the death of Jesus to pay the penalty for your sin so that you could be made right again (righteous) with Him in relationship. That's faith.

One of the problems that surfaced as the church was being formed was that people were hearing God's Word, but they were not putting it into practice—as if what God was saying was "optional." Sounds a lot like today's society, doesn't it? God's Word is the pathway to life, yet so many people treat it as one of many options to use if they feel it is relevant and beneficial for their particular circumstance. Hebrews 4:2 says, "But the message they heard was of no value to them, because they did not share the faith of those who obeyed."

If I am standing on one side of the street on a hot summer day and a man on the other side of the street offers free ice-cold lemonade, I have to put into action what I just heard and walk across the street in order to get the lemonade. Otherwise, knowing that the lemonade is offered is of no value to me. It only becomes valuable to me when I do something with it: when I walk across the street, take a cup, and drink it, quenching my thirst.

So it is with faith. Many people have gone to church all of their lives and have heard (and can even quote) great Scriptures from the Bible. Yet none of it held any value to them because they never put it into practice. It remains in their minds as intellectual knowledge, but it has had no profound effect on their lives.

Your Husband daily proves His faithfulness to you. He wants you confident enough and convinced enough to follow His lead even when you don't feel like it or understand it. You trust Him enough to know with certainty that His Word is true and His Spirit speaking to you is true, and therefore you will walk in that truth because you can trust Him.

Wrapping It Up

How brokenhearted I would feel if I possessed everything someone I loved needed to have the most joy-filled, exuberant life, and yet he would not allow me to give it to him. Your Husband has "everything [you] need for a godly life" (2 Peter 1:3), if you would trust Him enough to walk with Him and let Him lead, obeying what He tells you to do. That's why He put His Spirit in you. He wants you to hear His voice and follow Him as He leads you on the pathway to everlasting joy, peace, and love.

Loving Response

There's a scene in the Disney movie *Aladdin* where Aladdin confronts Jasmine with a question — "Do you trust me?" — as he extends his hand for her to step onto the magic carpet. At that moment, she can pull away or step into the scary unknown with deep trust. Your Husband is asking you the same question, "Do you trust Me?"

Seek Upwardly

Thank your Husband for being trustworthy. Ask Him to help you trust Him enough to walk in obedience to His Word even if it makes no sense.

Seek Inwardly

Your Husband has proven time and time again that He can be trusted, but today you need to wrestle with the question of whether you are living your life fully trusting in Him. Do you truly trust Him enough to let Him lead and control your life? Do you trust Him enough to obey His Word and His Spirit's promptings, even if they make no sense and you don't understand? All that He offers you will be of no value if it is not combined with your faith. It is not enough to say that you trust Him. You must act in a way that demonstrates your trust.

Seek Outwardly

Write Hebrews 4:2 from above in your journal. Then write "I Trust You" beside it. Journal to your Husband what is going on inside of your heart.

If you never have before, make today the first day to walk and talk with your Husband throughout the entire day. Periodically during the day, say to Him that you trust Him. This spiritual practice will remind you that He is present, and it will help you surrender your control moment by moment to the only One who deserves it.

Day 4: He Believes in You

Try again today to get outdoors in God's creation. Ask Him to reveal His presence to you and to teach you more about Him as you spend this time with Him.

. . . .

I can remember my very first opportunity to sing. I went with my youth director to a church and I was to sing prior to his preaching. I was so nervous! Right before I stood up to sing, my youth pastor said, "You can do this. God is with you and I believe in you." Something happens inside our souls when we hear empowering and inspiring words.

God is faithful to you, and I hope you are growing in your faith in Him. Here are another couple of thoughts to delve into today: Have you ever thought of the fact that He has faith in you? And as a result of that faith He has in you, are you faithful to Him?

Think about why a man marries a woman: because she is physically beautiful to him, because he sees her inner beauty that goes beyond outward appearance, because he enjoys her companionship, and because he sees her character and knows she would make a great partner for him. This is why God gave you to Jesus and why Jesus, your Husband, chose you and made a covenant with you. It is one thing to know that He is faithful and that you can have faith in Him. It is quite another to believe that He has faith in you! He believes in you!

When Jesus left this earth, He gave the Holy Spirit to those who would believe in Him by faith. The Spirit guides, leads, fills, comforts, and counsels people so that they might experience abundant life in covenant with Jesus and display Him accurately to the lost. And Jesus chose *you* for this incredible task! Why? Because He knows you and has faith in you. He confidently believes that by your yielding to the power of His Spirit, you can walk with Him in deeper intimacy, and you can do great things to convey to those around you the truth of who He is. Wow, what an empowering thought!

Open your Bible and read Matthew 5:14-16. Write in your journal what Jesus compared you to and what He empowers you to do.

> You are the light of the world. A town built on a hill cannot be hidden. Neither do people light a lamp and put it under a bowl. Instead they put it on its stand, and it gives light to everyone in the house. In the same way, let your light shine before others, that they may see your good deeds and glorify your Father in heaven.
> —Matthew 5:14-16

He is faithful. He offers you what you need to have faith. He has faith in you. But, are you faithful to Him?

Think of that word in terms of relationships, marriage, and affairs. To have an affair on your husband would be to say that you were "unfaithful" to him. Many couples are not even marrying anymore because they lack trust. They have seen their parents, even those who seemed godly and went to church regularly, divorce after years of marriage and have endured tremendous pain as a result. They want no part of marriage and have even declared that no one can truly be trusted anymore. They feel the best viable option is just to live together. That way, they make no long-term commitment, and any time the relationship gets uncomfortable, they can just get out.

If anyone is worthy of our faithfulness, it would be Jesus. He has proven His faithfulness, He has given you the Holy Spirit to help you live by faith, and He has shown that He has faith in you to accomplish all that He created you to do. All He asks is that you remain faithful to Him in return.

Are you having an affair on your Husband? Does your love for the things and people of this world overshadow your love for Him? Do you truly trust Him or are you just co-habiting with Him without any commitment to walk by His Spirit's leading or to obey Him? Have you controlled and positioned the relationship so that you can get out whenever you get uncomfortable? I am not asking if you are saved. I am asking if you really trust Him or not. Is He really your Husband—the One to whom you are eternally committed, openly proclaiming, and willingly obeying? Is He the Lord of your life? Really? Are you just living with God or are you married to Him?

Wrapping It Up

God believes in you. God trusts that you will take His Light to the darkness in this world. He is faithful to you, but He also has faith *in* you! He wants you to be faithful in return, by being the Light of Christ to those who desperately need Him.

Loving Response

Seek Upwardly

Sit before your Husband and talk with Him about where you two are in relationship. Confess if you have been "living with Him" but not fully committed to Him. Confess your lack of trust because of others who proved unworthy of trust. Recommit yourself in covenant with Him. Surrender your life afresh and anew to Him in complete trust. Meditate on this promise from Psalm 146:6: "[The Lord] remains faithful forever."

Seek Inwardly

Journal your heart to Him. Talk with Him about your insecurities when it comes to stepping out in faith and living completely for Him. Ask for His grace to help you.

Seek Outwardly

If you have access to the song "Love Came Down" by Kari Jobe, play it now and make the words a song of commitment to your Husband.

Day 5: Gave to Give

Find one last quiet place for you and God out in His creation. Maybe God has spoken to you in such a powerful way as you have sat outside with Him that you will continue to do that beyond this study. Ask Him to guide you and speak to you as you continue your journey of discovering who He really is.

· · · · · · · · ·

It has been the desire of my heart to invite you on a journey with God and to show you who He really is. My prayer is not that you learned more, but that you engaged your Husband more, and have plunged into deeper intimacy with Him. I also pray that you have been awakened to the leading of the Holy Spirit (who your Husband put in you to remind you of His presence and incomprehensible love).

Maybe over the course of these weeks, you have seen how you have made other relationships more of a priority than your relationship with God. The best way you can "affair-proof" your relationship with Him is to fill yourself so full of His presence and love that there is no room for anything or anybody else. It's kind of like Thanksgiving dinner. Your mother fixes the best food with all of the trimmings and you eat until you have taken that final and sometimes fatal bite that screams, "Don't put another piece of food in here or you will be sorry!" About the time you sit down to let your stuffed tummy settle, here comes your mother with your very favorite pie. Though you may want it, you have to turn it down because you are so completely satisfied and there is just no room for anything else. Be this way with your Husband and He will so satisfy you that there will be no room for anything or anyone else to take His rightful place.

Let's look at John 3:16 one more time. Even if you have memorized it, find it in your Bible and read it.

> For God so loved the world that he gave his one and only Son, that whoever believes in him shall not perish but have eternal life. — John 3:16

So often, I have focused on the overall message in this passage, but there is so much more to explore. God so loved that He gave. Because of the depth of His love for you and me, He gave the very best He had. He gave us a Groom who would storm the castle to save us. But why? Why would He give so much? God gave us a Groom so that He could keep on giving to us. Jesus gave Himself so that He could continually give never-ending abundant life to us.

Think about it: No one has been with you since the very beginning of your life, and no one will continue to be with you for eternity except your Husband, your Lover, your Groom. No one. He has always been present, always been pursuing you, always been keeping His promises to you. He is continually perfecting you and partnering with you. He has always been passionate about you and will be permanently with you and for you — forever. He gave Himself, so He could continue to give you the happy, fulfilled, free, full, and joyful life that He planned for you since the day of your conception. He gave to keep on giving. Amazing love.

Maybe you have never experienced or understood the One True God in His fullness like this. Maybe it's time you asked for a divorce from the man-made gods that others created for you or you created for yourself. God is calling you to return to Him, the Lover of your soul who created you and loves you with a love you cannot fathom nor deserve. No matter what you've done — how you've blamed Him, walked away from Him, thought your way was better than His — He has never, never, never stopped loving you. Never. This is the essence of faithfulness. This is the essence of God. God has offered you His unfailing, never-ending, faithful love long before the day of your first breath. He has never stopped loving you and He never will. He gave

His life so that He could spend eternity with you, where He can continually lavish His love on you, face to face.

> For now we see in a mirror dimly, but then face to face. Now I know in part; then I shall know fully, even as I [all this time] have been fully known. (1 Corinthians 13:12, ESV)

Wrapping It Up

When the final curtain on your life has been drawn and life in your physical body comes to an end, you will fall asleep in the arms of your Groom and awaken in His presence—face to face. Psalm 17:15 says, "[I] will see your face; when I awake, I will be satisfied with seeing your likeness." No more tears, no more struggles, no more failures, no more fear, no more sorrow or regrets. You will be like Him, just the way He originally created you: happy, fulfilled, and free, where you will enjoy His loving presence, and you will live happily ever after.

Loving Response

Seek Upwardly

Listen to the song "Never Once" by Matt Redman; you may even want to record the words in your journal as a statement of praise to your faithful Husband.

Seek Inwardly

Journal your heart to God. Look back at all of these weeks you've spent together and how your view of Him has changed. Tell Him what He means to you. Tell Him how you have grown to know and love Him more and more. Respond to all that He truly is to you. Thank Him that He is no longer an "unknown" god to you, but that you know Him as He truly is. Thank Him for your time together and ask Him to prepare you and guide you for what comes next on your journey together.

Seek Outwardly

Take the time to share with some of your friends what you have learned about God. If some might be interested in learning more about who God is, offer to take them through this study, so that they can have a more intimate relationship with Him and find that He is their Husband too.

Think about what you have learned about who God is throughout this study. Seek to capture that in a picture, song lyrics, or art. Bring your work and your journal with you to your next group meeting so you can share all that God is doing in your heart and life.

Thank you for joining me for the Love study! If you would like to stay connnected with me as you continue your path of discipleship, I would love to hear from you and how this study impacted your life! Simply go to www.livingdeeperministries.com and join a host of other women who want to be disciples of Jesus and take others with them! There, you will find great encouragement for your journey with Jesus.

Surrendered,
Jena

how to become a christian

This section may be the most important one you read in this entire book. Everything else that is written will not compare to what God will do through your life as you surrender to Him. No life will ever reach the heights intended unless one is born again. Read below, talk to God, and follow Him by accepting Jesus as your Lord. After you decide to follow Jesus, you will never be the same again. May God transform you into the person He desires for you to be as you allow Jesus to become the Savior of your soul and the Lord of your life.

Recognize That God Loves You

> For God so loved the world that he gave his one and only Son, that whoever believes in him shall not perish but have eternal life. (John 3:16)

Recognize That You Have Sinned

> For all have sinned and fall short of the glory of God. (Romans 3:23)

Recognize That Sin's Debt Must Be Paid

For the wages of sin is death, but the gift of God is eternal life in Christ Jesus our Lord. (Romans 6:23)

Recognize That Christ Paid for Your Sins

But God demonstrates his own love for us in this: While we were still sinners, Christ died for us. (Romans 5:8)

Pray and Receive Christ Today

Everyone who calls on the name of the Lord will be saved. (Romans 10:13)

For he says,

> "In the time of my favor I heard you,
> and in the day of salvation I helped you."

I tell you, now is the time of God's favor, now is the day of salvation. (2 Corinthians 6:2)

Today, you can receive Jesus as your Lord and Savior.

As you agree with the Scriptures above, simply pray this prayer aloud:

Dear Jesus, I invite You to forgive me of my sins and come into my heart and life right now. I receive Your gift of payment of my sins by dying in my place.

I accept You, Jesus, as my Lord and Savior. Please reveal Yourself to me and become real in my life from this moment forward. Thank

You for saving me and giving me eternal life. I love You and commit
my life to You. Amen.

What to Do Now?

I want to encourage you to do the following three things as a response
to your decision:

1. Tell someone. Tell a close friend, your spouse, and even tell
   me! I would love to hear from you about your decision to
   follow Jesus! E-mail me at jena@livingdeeperministries.com
   and let me know!
2. Find a church home that will baptize you and nurture you in
   your new walk with the Lord.
3. Commit to grow daily in your new Christian life by reading
   the Bible, praying, and having fellowship with other believers.

notes

A Note from the Author

1. Donald Miller, *Searching for God Knows What* (Nashville: Thomas Nelson, 2004), 25.

Week 1: A Match Made in Heaven

1. A. W. Tozer, *The Attributes of God*, vol. 1 (Camp Hill, PA: WingSpread Publishers, 2001), 124–125.
2. Susan E. Isaacs, *Angry Conversations with God* (New York: FaithWords, 2009), 26–27.

Week 3: Tying the Knot

1. www.dictionary.com, s.v. "sacred."
2. Christy Nockels and Nathan Nockels, "Seek Me" (Word Music, 2001).
3. Abraham Cohen, *Everyman's Talmud* (New York: Schocken Publishing, 1995); Louis M. Epstein, *The Jewish Marriage Contract* (New York: Jewish Theological Seminary of America, 1927), 78–79; Bill Risk, "The Ultimate Wedding," May 15, 1996, http://www.ldolphin.org/risk/ult.shtml.

about the author

JENA FOREHAND experienced firsthand God's power to transform a life when He healed her broken marriage in 1997. With a spirit of authenticity, Jena and her husband, Dale, began ministering to other couples through marriage conferences, retreats, and resources. She was next drawn to women's ministry and the incredible need for living in deeper relationship with God through discipleship.

Jena's passion for Christ is evident as she writes and speaks clearly, comically, and candidly to women. When not traveling with her husband and family, she focuses her time and energy on how to best partner with future generations in discipleship. Jena lives in Birmingham, Alabama, with her family.

God Is.....
Present
Pursueing
Promise - Keeper
Perfecter
Partner
Passionate

Let people off the hook for
living perfect!
Spirit of God is teacher.
The Word Believe = to place your
confidence in; give oneself fully to.
Belly - glutton - womb - conceived
Soul - feelings + emotions.

John 7:38